OSPREY COMBAT AIRCRAFT • 59

F-15E STRIKE EAGLE UNITS IN COMBAT 1990–2005

SERIES EDITOR: TONY HOLMES

OSPREY COMBAT AIRCRAFT • 59

F-15E STRIKE EAGLE UNITS IN COMBAT 1990–2005

STEVE DAVIES

OSPREY
PUBLISHING

Front cover
In the wake of the 11 September 2001 terrorist attacks on New York and Washington, DC, F-15Es from the 391st FS/366th Air Expeditionary Wing (AEW), based at Mountain Home, deployed to Kuwait for Operation *Enduring Freedom* (OEF). During the course of their three-month tenure, four crewmen from the unit entered the history books when they flew the longest fighter combat sortie ever (no exact date for this mission has ever been released by the USAF).

For 15.5 hours – nine of which were spent over the target – 'Crockett 51' and '52' were assigned to patrol a set of grid coordinates over Afghanistan for the usual 'vulnerability' time of three hours. In the lead aircraft were 'Slokes' and 'Snitch' (pilot and WSO) and in the second F-15E were 'Spear' and 'Buzzer'. Each aircraft carried nine GBU-12 500-lb LGBs, two AIM-9M and two AIM-120C air-to-air missiles and two wing fuel tanks.

Once on-station, 'Crockett' flight received a time sensitive target from their AWACS controller, who told them to contact a Predator drone control unit that had been monitoring suspicious activity around a set of buildings believed to be Taliban command and control facilities. Once communication with the Predator had been established, 'Crockett' flight was instructed to strike both buildings. 'Spear' recalled what happened next;

'Each jet set up two different laser codes. "Crockett 51" had 1511 on the left CFT (conformal fuel tank) and 1533 on the right, while "Crockett 52" had 1522 on the left and 1544 on the right. "Crockett 51" released four GBU-12s, giving us two with the 1511 laser code and two with 1533. We programmed in 1533 on our laser so that we could guide two of the bombs and they had 1511 dialled in on theirs so that they could guide the other two LGBs. This way we took out two buildings, side-by-side, with simultaneous impacts. We actually flew two passes – the first to ensure that we had the correct targets, and the second to actually drop the weapons.'

Both targets were neutralised effectively (*Cover artwork by Mark Postlethwaite*)

For those who made the ultimate sacrifice – Capt Eric 'Boot' Das, Maj William R 'Salty' Watkins III, Lt Col William E Morel III, Capt Jeffrey K 'Flounder' Fahnlander, Capt Dennis White, Maj Bruce 'Phoid' Netardus, Lt Col Wendell 'Sheik' Johnson, Maj Thomas F 'Teek' Koritz, Lt Col Donnie R 'Chief Dimpled Balls' Holland, Maj Peter S Hook and Capt James B 'Boo Boo' Poulet

First published in Great Britain in 2005 by Osprey Publishing
Midland House, West Way, Botley, Oxford OX2 0PH, UK
443 Park Avenue South, New York, NY 10016, USA
E-mail:info@ospreypublishing.com

ISBN 1 84176 909 6

Edited by Tony Holmes
Page design by Tony Truscott
Cover Artwork by Mark Postlethwaite
Aircraft Profiles by Chris Davey
Index by Alan Thatcher
Originated by PPS-Grasmere, Leeds, UK
Printed in China through Bookbuilders

05 06 07 08 09   10 09 08 07 06 05 04 03 02 01

For a catalogue of all books published by Osprey please contact:
NORTH AMERICA
Osprey direct, 2427 Bond Street, University Park, IL 60466, USA
E-mail: info@ospreydirectusa,com

ALL OTHER REGIONS
Osprey Direct UK, P.O. Box 140 Wellingborough, Northants, NN8 2FA, UK
E-mail: info@ospreydirect.co.uk
www.ospreypublishing.com

ACKNOWLEDGEMENTS
The author would like to thank the following for their help in the production of this volume: Brig Gen Mark Matthews, Lt Cols James McCullough, Michael Arnold, Will Reece and Gary Klett, Majs John Donahue, Bernadette Dozier and Mike Neeman, Capts Chris Russell, Randy Haskin and Ed Ekpoudom, Lts Jamie Humphries and Toni Tones, Sgt Will Ackerman, TSgt Kathleen Cordner and Al Gale. Finally, special thanks go to Lt Col Jerry Oney, who was always quick to answer questions, put me in touch with his squadronmates from *Desert Storm*, and who sent his entire photo collection 4000 miles 'across the pond' so that I could include some unique and original images in Chapter 2.

CONTENTS

F-15E OVERVIEW

The F-15E Strike Eagle is the dedicated multi-role adaptation of the original F-15 Eagle air superiority airframe, and it has matured into the most capable, well-rounded, strike fighter of all time. Its development came about as a result of a combination of clever corporate strategy by McDonnell Douglas, the foresight and vision of USAF Tactical Air Command (TAC) commander Gen Wilbur Creech and the ageing status of the F-111.

Defence contractors McDonnell Douglas and Hughes recognised that a two-seat dedicated strike version of the F-15 might be of great interest to the US Air Force, and set about developing this concept under the internal project name 'Strike Eagle'. The consortium received positive encouragement from Gen Creech, who worried that as the F-111 grew older, TAC would lose its edge in the deep strike role. This was a crucial mission in Western Europe, which was then firmly in the grip of the Cold War. USAFE was tasked with carrying out the deep strike role with a complement of over 100 F-111E/Fs, split between two British-based tactical fighter wings at RAF Lakenheath (48th TFW) and RAF Upper Heyford (20th TFW), respectively.

Savaged by the world's media in its early years, the F-111 had been developed into a potent strike platform that offered long range, terrain following and precision strike capabilities. The Pave Tack pod on the F-111F used infrared imaging to enable the crew to visually acquire their targets at night, and it could also fire a laser onto the target to allow Laser Guided Bombs (LGBs) to home in on the reflected laser energy and strike with pinpoint accuracy. The Terrain Following Radar (TFR) gave the crew the ability to fly down to a height of just 200 ft in all weathers, thereby avoiding enemy radar and visual detection.

Building on the USAF's operational experience with the F-111, Hughes quickly realised that the F-15C's fighter-optimised radar would need to be significantly modified if the new Strike Eagle was going to surpass the performance of the Pave Tack-equipped F-111F. The corporation duly went back to the drawing board with a view to completely overhauling and improving the F-15C's APG-63 radar for the

The Strike Eagle began life as a natural follow-on from the air superiority F-15A/C Eagle. Utilising avionics space, systems compatibility and wiring that had been deliberately built into the Eagle for air-to-ground purposes, F-15B 71-0291 was used as the test bed for development. The jet is seen here carrying a full load of Mk 7 Rockeye Cluster Bomb Units on its CFT pylons. The aircraft also bears the Advanced Fighter Capability Demonstrator badge on its fins. 71-0291 remained with the manufacturer until retired in May 1999, after which it served in the airframe battle damage repair role at Warner-Robins AFB (*Boeing via Author*)

Strike Eagle. The end result was the APG-70, complete with Synthetic Aperture Radar (SAR). The latter measures the Doppler Shift created when radar waves hit the ground and bounce back to the antenna.

Using complex computer algorithms to establish the movement of the aircraft relative to the ground, the APG-70 interprets these shifts and translates them into a top-down picture in the two-seat cockpit. The resulting image gives a clear view of the ground, which, when viewed by the pilot or Weapons Systems Officer (WSO), looks similar to a bird's eye view of the target area. This process is known as 'patch-mapping', and can be achieved down to a resolution of 0.67th of a nautical mile.

Two other key components were integrated into the Strike Eagle – the Conformal Fuel Tank (CFT) and LANTIRN (Low Altitude Navigation Targeting Infra Red for Night). CFTs were slipper tanks that mounted flush along the aircraft's side, below the wing root. They carried extra fuel and also featured weapons hard points to allow additional stores to be carried.

The USAF had signed a contract with Martin Marietta to produce the LANTIRN system, which was a combination of forward-looking infrared optics and TFR that would eventually be mounted below the engine nacelles in two underslung pods. LANTIRN reached operational status in 1987.

Designated the AAQ-13 Navigation Pod and AAQ-14 Target Pod (TP), each was attached to the aircraft via two mounted lugs and simple electrical terminals. The 'Nav Pod' housed a FLIR sensor and TFR, and was primarily used by the pilot to allow hands-off low altitude flying in all weather, night or day. The FLIR sensor looked ahead of the aircraft and could display the resulting image onto the pilot's Kaiser-built, Wide Field of View (WFOV) Head-Up Display (HUD). The TFR looked ahead and slightly to either side of the jet to detect obstacles and terrain.

Mounted on the left pylon, the TP was used by the WSO to identify and designate targets when weather conditions permitted, and could be either cued to the radar or manipulated independently. It had three selectable Fields Of View and housed a laser designator with which to guide LGBs onto the target. The WSO then had to find his target in the TP, put the cross hairs over it and press a button to commit the pod to

F-15B 71-0291 shed its fighter greys for a two-tone 'slime green' scheme when it became time for its initial demonstrations and Dual Role Fighter trials with the USAF. The one-off camouflage scheme made the jet look much more the part, as did a weapons load-out of 16 Mk 82 bombs (*Boeing via Author*)

tracking it. Several tracking options were available, all of which permitted the WSO to keep one eye on other systems during the course of the attack run – something that F-111F WSOs were never able to do.

The F-15E was also modified to allow a 16,000-hour fatigue life, the forward avionics bays were redesigned and the ammunition carriage space for the M61A1 Vulcan cannon was reduced in size to make way for additional avionics. The engine bays were also modified to allow commonality in plumbing and installation for either the Pratt & Whitney F100 or General Electric F110 engines, whilst the tail hook was strengthened to accommodate a heavier anticipated landing weight.

These various modifications gave the Strike Eagle a new sustained 9g capability, but compelled the installation of a new landing gear and wheels in order to allow the jet to operate safely at higher gross weights. The F-15E weighed almost 16,000 lbs more than the F-15C when empty, and had a maximum take-off weight of 81,000 lbs, compared with 58,470 lbs for the C-model fitted with external fuel tanks.

The aircraft's two-seat cockpit was considerably modified from that fitted into the fighter-optimised F-15D, with the emphasis being placed on interoperability. Both crewmembers had to be able to perform almost any function necessary to get the mission done. The front cockpit featured two monochrome multi purpose displays (MPD) and one colour MPD (MPCD), while the rear cockpit housed two MPDs and two MPCDs. An up front controller (UFC) was installed in each cockpit to allow the crew to enter data into the sophisticated avionics suite.

PRODUCTION AND SERVICE INTRODUCTION

Following a six-month competition against the General Dynamics F-16XL, the F-15E was ordered into production in 1984 after it was chosen by the USAF as a replacement for the F-111 in 1984. On 11 December 1986 the first of three full scale development F-15Es (86-0183) make its maiden flight, followed shortly afterwards by two others (86-0184 and 86-0185).

With the completion of operational trials with the F-15C-equipped 33rd TFW at Eglin AFB, the first of the USAF's 236 production examples was delivered to the 405th Tactical Training Wing at Luke AFB in 1988. In December of that same year the 4th TFW at Seymour Johnson AFB began its conversion from the F-4E to the F-15E. The wing would not have to wait long to prove the Strike Eagle's ability in combat.

The first of three full scale development F-15Es departs McDonnell Douglas's St Louis home on an early test flight in December 1986. This aircraft was the first Strike Eagle to be painted in the now-familiar charcoal grey scheme which has adorned every F-15E built since. Assigned to the USAF's test wing at Edwards AFB until 1997, the jet (86-0183) is presently a part of Boeing's St Louis-based test fleet, where it is involved in Strike Eagle-related development projects (*Boeing via Author*)

DESERT SHIELD AND DESERT STORM

As the first wing to fly the Strike Eagle operationally, the 4th TFW at Seymour Johnson AFB began planning its inaugural F-15E Operational Readiness Exercise (ORE) in July 1990. The ORE would take the few Mission Ready (MR) 335th Tactical Fighter Squadron (TFS) 'Chiefs' crews and mix them and their jets with those of the 336th TFS 'Rocketeers' to form a 'Rainbow package' – Rainbow because of the mixed tail stripe colours. The package also included F-4Es from the 334th TFS 'Eagles', which had yet to convert to the F-15E.

The ORE objective was to demonstrate the wing's ability to utilise the electronic attack, navigation and target designation systems on the F-15E to place precision strikes on a range of targets over a short period of time. It was almost with a sense of prophecy, therefore, that 4th TFW Intelligence dreamt up the scenario that saw the Iraqi Army invade Kuwait! The Strike Eagles would simulate penetrating heavily-defended terrain in order to bring down bridges and other logistics choke points to halt the enemy advance.

The 'Rainbow package' flew for 11 days straight, each pilot and WSO often completing two or more sorties per day, culminating in the last day of the ORE (2 August) when 24 aircraft made their way north to 'attack' Virginia's bridges. That same day, the Strike Eagle crews, and the rest of the world, watched aghast as Iraqi President Saddam Hussein ordered his troops to invade Kuwait.

Within hours the 'Rocketeers' were given the order to prepare to deploy, but 335th TFS crews, of whom only a third were mission ready, were not expected to go. One week later, on 9 August 1990, four six-ship flights of F-15Es and 48 crewmen began deploying to Seeb AB, in Oman – a journey requiring a 15-hour non-stop flight, which started at Seymour Johnson in atrocious weather. During the transit, the jets' destination was changed to the Omani air base at Thumrait. Lt Col Gary Klett (then a captain) recalled;

'I had about 600 hours in the F-4 when I was selected to convert to the F-15E. I left for the RTU (replacement training unit) at Luke AFB on the same day that the 336th FS F-15Es deployed to Oman. The whole time we were going through the conversion we kept one eye on CNN to see if we could spot any of the gang on TV.

'I got home from Luke just before Christmas 1990, but I didn't hurry back because I didn't think I had a chance in hell of going when the

"Chiefs" deployed, even though I had orders to the squadron. I wouldn't have enough time to complete mission qualification training (MQT) before they left, and there were about six or eight of us in the same situation. I was sure all of us would get told to report next door to the 334th TFS "Eagles", since it was still in the process of converting and would therefore not be deploying.'

Upon arrival at Thumrait, in Oman, the 336th TFS's F-15Es immediately assumed alert. WSO Maj Jerry Oney (right, seen here posing with his pilot Capt Bill 'Shadow' Schaal), who was amongst the crews deployed right at the start of *Desert Shield*, recalled 'Things were somewhat uncertain at the time as to who might come across which border and try their hand against us, so we had a bunch of different configurations'. The brand new jets – many with less than 200-hours in their logbooks – that had been sent from Seymour Johnson sported either four AIM-9 Sidewinders and four AIM-7 Sparrows, or four AIM-9s and twelve Mk 20 Rockeye CBUs or twelve Mk 82 LDGBs. This aircraft features the all-missile alert fit *(Jerry Oney via Author)*

Operation *Desert Shield*, the precursor to Operation *Desert Storm*, began with the deployment of F-15C/Es to the Persian Gulf region. On 9 August the 336th TFS F-15Es flew into Thumrait AB, via Dhahran, in Saudi Arabia, the base in Oman already boasting stockpiles of weapons that had been stored by the USAF for just such an eventuality.

Initially, confusion reigned within the 336th, as the unit, operating as the 4th TFW (Provisional) and led by Col Russell 'Rusty' Bolt, was without clear orders or directives. The reality of its situation was stark. Nine Iraqi Republican Guard units stood ready at the Kuwaiti border to steamroller south into Saudi Arabia, whose oil fields might also be in the sights of the Iraqi dictator. It quickly became evident that the 'Rocketeers' were the only force that could delay and harass such an advance, although the price they might pay in the process did not bear thinking about.

By 11 August the unit had 12 jets on alert, although this had not been achieved without considerable effort. Capt Mike 'Smy' Smyth arrived in-theatre on Christmas Day 1990, and he recalled that the F-15E was only cleared to release 500-lb Mk 82 and 2000-lb Mk 84 LDGP (Low Drag General Purpose) bombs at that time, although other weapons had been tested by the *Seek Eagle* testing programme at Eglin AFB.

It was with some consternation, therefore, that the unit contemplated dropping the Mk 20 Rockeye Cluster Bomb Unit (CBU) from the jet, as it had not been fully tested from all weapons stations. These concerns were more than valid, as some crews had seen release test video footage of the Strike Eagle prototype being struck by a 500-lb bomb that had just been released from a CFT and whipped back up behind the wing into the horizontal stabiliser.

This aircraft, on the other hand, stands on alert with four AIM-9s and twelve Mk 20 Rockeye CBUs at the ready *(USAF)*

The Mk 20 Rockeye was an 'area munition' that released hundreds of cricket ball-size bomblets over an area as large as a football field, and was therefore far more effective in killing lightly armoured targets than LDGPs. The Air Force waived normal procedures and permitted the 336th to load 'unauthorised' stores onto the jet. The Mk 20 could now also be added to the F-15E's arsenal.

Maj Jerry Oney snapped this photograph shortly after the 336th TFS had arrived in Thumrait. 'This group shot was taken at Oman after we'd been there for a month or so. We are standing on the ramp where we parked our jets that we loaded up for alert. Virtually everyone had been working out pretty hard during that time, so guys were only too happy to sport their "new look"! The gym facilities were modest on base, but we all got in pretty good shape. Almost all of the officers in our squadron are present in this photo, including our Intel and ops-admin guys' (*Jerry Oney via Author*)

Two Strike Eagles also stood ready to defend the base, or a strike package, from enemy attack, and these were loaded with AIM-7 Sparrow and AIM-9 Sidewinder missiles.

Morale in the squadron soon ebbed away as the crews sat for two weeks without full communication with Central Command Air Force (CENTAF) HQ in Riyadh. This left the unit effectively grounded, being unable to fly unless Iraqi armour mobilised once again. Lt Col Bolt added to these problems by imposing a 300-ft minimum altitude training limit when the squadron did return to flying. Under considerable pressure not to lose an aircraft – the pre-eminent preoccupation of any wing commander – Bolt was probably fearful that losing jets in training would not only have a detrimental impact on the squadron's ability to protect Saudi Arabia, but also lose him his command.

The training limit was subsequently broken by many of the crews, who felt that they needed to be below 200 ft if they were to survive the dense and coordinated network of Surface to Air Missiles (SAM) and Anti Aircraft Artillery (AAA) fielded by Iraq. This insubordination ultimately cost at least one pilot his wings.

Ironically, it was at this time that F-15E 87-0203 was lost on a sortie that had nothing to do with low-level flying. The Strike Eagle had been flying intercepts against a pair of RAF Jaguar GR 1s when it ploughed into the desert on 30 September with the loss of its pilot, Maj Pete Hook, and WSO, Capt Jim Poulet. Although a full investigation into the incident was never carried out, it is possible that inexperience in handling the F-15E with external fuel tanks was the primary cause of the accident.

Al Gale, a WSO with the 'Rocke-teers', elucidated:

'Aircrews are taught the various sensory illusions that can deceive you when flying. One of them is a lack of depth perception for your altitude when you are flying over a nondescript surface such as a smooth ocean or flat desert. The desert in the Middle East was extremely bad in this respect. The surface was often completely

Two 336th TFS jets depart Thumrait on an early training sortie in the autumn of 1990. Lacking bombs, these aircraft are both equipped with AAQ-13 TFR pods, however (*USAF*)

smooth sand with no vegetation at all. It looked exactly the same whether you were flying at 300 ft or 30,000 ft. Flying at night over the southern part of Saudi Arabia looked just like flying over the ocean. Although we were over the land, there were no visible lights as far as the eye could see in all directions. The only way to tell your altitude was to look at the altimeter, whether it be day or night. Pete and Jim were fine aviators, and their loss was both a shock and very sad for all of us'.

This loss was followed by the fatal crashes of an RF-4C (8 October) and an F-111F (11 October), both at low level. CENTAF HQ consequently issued a diktat directing that all aircraft, with the exception of the B-52, were forthwith restricted to a 500-ft minimum training altitude. It was greeted by F-15E crews with a mixture of exasperation and incredulity.

Tactics subsequently determined in impromptu meetings by senior squadron staff proved ironic, as they consisted primarily of the 'Pop' manoeuvre, which had previously been banned due to its risky nature. Dive and Dive-Toss methods were viewed as alternatives, although the medium-altitude SAM threat would probably make these unrealistic options. A hastily created Mission Planning Cell (MPC) did what it could to prepare the aircrews for war, but a centralised input was really needed.

Back at Seymour Johnson, the 336th's Capt Gary Klett was still working his way through the F-15E MQT;

'About eight days before Christmas I was told by the squadron Ops Officer to get my mobility gear in order because I was going to the Middle East after all. He explained, "You won't get to fly over there, but you can assist with mission planning and generally help out". "Okay, that's better than sitting over here and watching the 'bro's' do the whole thing on CNN", I thought. So, along with three or four other guys in the same MQT situation, I soon found myself on my way to Saudi Arabia on 26 December 1990. We named ourselves the "MQ Maggots" in reference to the fact that we hadn't completed MQT. However, once we arrived at Al Kharj and the bosses got a good look at the wartime frag orders, it became apparent that everyone was going to be needed to fill the large number of planned sorties. It just broke our hearts!

F-15E 86-1694 of the 336th TFS heads out on yet another training flight at dusk from Thumrait during *Desert Shield*. Delivered to the 4th TFW on 14 February 1990, this aircraft served exclusively with the 336th up until it was sent to the Warner Robins Air Logistics Center in March 1998 for overhaul and upgrading. Issued to the 335th FS upon its return to Seymour Johnson, the F-15E deployed to Al Udeid with the unit for Operation *Iraqi Freedom* in February 2003. Two months later, on 7 April, the jet became the 4th FW's sole combat loss of OIF when it crashed whilst supporting Special Forces north of Tikrit. Both the pilot, Capt Eric Das, and WSO, Maj William Watkins, were killed (*USAF*)

The difficulties encountered by crews when flying at low level over featureless and barren desert landscapes were easy to underestimate. The main problem stemmed from the lack of depth perception and an inability to accurately judge altitude when flying over the desert floor (*Jerry Oney via Author*)

'Prior to the war starting, there were relatively few training sorties available, and the guys who were already mission qualified got most of those. I ended up with only one training sortie prior to hostilities – a night "let's see what they're gonna' do" sortie. We would set up a few flights outside of Saddam's radar coverage then run at the border and see what his air defence guys would do when several flights were detected making a run straight towards them. It sounds like more fun than it was. For us, it was just a couple hours of relative boredom. The worst thing was that it didn't allow me any practice doing the things I'd have to do on an attack.'

Capt Jerry 'One-Y' Oney, who was a WSO with the 'Rocketeers' at the time, remembered;

'I had the good fortune to be crewed with Capt Bill "Shadow" Schaal during most of my sorties in *Desert Shield* and *Desert Storm*. The strange thing is that I'd never even met Bill until we all showed up at Thumrait. By my second flight with him it was pretty clear that he was a great stick, and ought to go to weapons school one of these days, which he eventually did. Flying with the same guy all the time is the only way to go in combat, although we were probably like an old married couple by the time the war was over. We pretty much had the run of Oman, and conducted some great training during the time we were there. We flew a number of low-level sorties, and some of the scenery – when you had time to enjoy it, which wasn't often – was spectacular.'

TACC

Back in Riyadh, CENTAF and Coalition representatives formed the Tactical Air Control Centre (TACC), which set about planning the air war as defined by a 600-page document called the Air Tasking Order (ATO). The ATO was the route map for the air campaign against Iraq, and it detailed every sortie that was to be flown. The F-15Es were to operate in unison with F-4G Wild Weasels and EF-111 jamming aircraft against SAM sites and key airfield complexes, but they were also assigned to the most politically problematic target of them all – Scuds.

Iraq operated four Scud types, all based on the original Soviet SS-1 missile, which was a surface-launched weapon of not particularly great accuracy with a range of over 200 miles. Iraq had adapted the Scud's warhead to carry chemical or biological loads, and showed no hesitation in using them against neighbouring countries. Doing so could upset the entire balance of neutrality of other Arab nations in the region (Jordan, Syria etc.), and so the Scud threat was to be neutralised at all costs.

In respect to launch sites, Iraq had both fixed batteries, which could be attacked with ease, and mobile units. The latter posed the greatest concern, and ultimately proved very nearly impossible to locate.

Capt Mike Smyth was seconded as the 'Rocketeers'' Fighter Duty Officer (FIDO) to the TACC for part of the war, although he later flew combat missions too. He explained;

'As the F-15E FIDO, I was the Strike Eagle representative at the TACC. Any questions about F-15E capabilities, tactics, range and payload were directed at me. I also helped coordinate take-off times, refuelling times and locations. I would work closely with the aircrew, often talking over the telephone to the flight leads before they briefed and took off.

Lt Col Bill Hopewell fills out pre-flight paperwork in the mission planning room at Thumrait in October 1990. Hopewell was the 336th TFS's Operations Officer during the first two months of *Desert Shield*, and he was instrumental in helping the unit deploy to Oman and quickly settle into life in-theatre. Hopewell had rotated back to Seymour Johnson by the time the 'Rocketeers' moved to Al Kharj, in Saudi Arabia
(Jerry Oney via Author)

'I had two telephones on my desk, one of which was a hotline to a sergeant in the command post who would pass me all the actual take-off and landing times. My discussions with the flight leads usually centred on coordination times, locations and call-signs for the other flights (usually EF-111s or F-4Gs) who would be in the area. I often had to pass new coordinates or target descriptions over the telephone due to changes in the plan frag. Another example of last minute coordination was moving the pre-strike or post-strike refuelling location, or coordinating for more fuel.

'The TACC was located in downtown Riyadh in one of the Ministry of Defence buildings. I worked the night shift from 1900 to 0700 hrs, but you could never just show up at the start of your shift and "have your finger on the pulse" and be ready to run the air war. I almost always worked 1800 to 0800 hrs in order to ensure a good hand-off from my day shift counterpart. This provided a 1.5-2.0 hour overlap in our shift, which was always necessary to have a good feel for what had happened while you were sleeping.

'There was an 0800 hrs briefing every morning, where we gathered all the night's statistics – number of sorties, targets hit/missed, maintenance aborts, etc. This briefing was another reason for the overlap in FIDO shifts.'

In December the 'Rocketeers' and 'Chiefs' moved to Al Kharj AB, in Saudi Arabia, following the realisation that the Iraqis were not going to advance any further south. Jerry Oney recalled this base change;

'We moved up to "Al's Garage" and got all settled in up there. This was good and bad. Good in the sense that the flying time to Iraq was considerably shortened, but bad in the fact that we moved into tents from hard billets with real flush toilets. The "Shitter Tents" at "Al's Garage" were a real treat as long as you didn't mind crapping in front of a crowd. Yeah, we're not gonna' get too much sympathy from our ground-buddies on that one.'

Maj Jerry 'One-y' Oney takes a break in order to catch up with the news in the 'Rocketeers'' squadron building at Thumrait. He told the author, 'Believe it or not we didn't have access to all that much news from the outside world. One guy had a radio which we were able to listen to occasionally, and we were able to make calls back to the States on the Thumrait Officers' Club telephone. One of the guys set up a schedule – rigidly adhered to – in which we were able to make a 15-minute call home. The calls started around midnight and were made seven days a week' *(Jerry Oney via Author)*

Maj Jerry Oney (left) and Lt Col Bob 'Mongo' Gruver pose in festive garb, along with an Operation *Desert Shield* bumper sticker that Oney's wife Karen had sent her husband. This F-15E is loaded with Mk 20 Rockeye CBUs for close air support *(Jerry Oney via Author)*

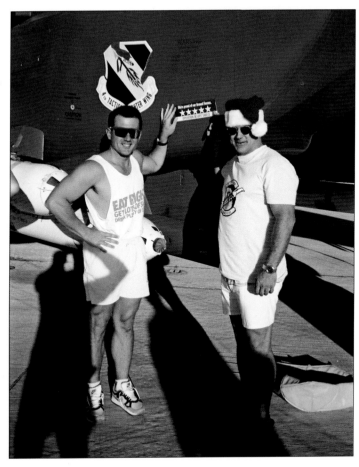

336th TFS jets sit on the ramp at Al Kharj, in Saudi Arabia, soon after arriving at the base in December 1990 – note the C-5 Galaxy climbing away from the base. The large concrete wall in the distance separated the 4th TFW(P)'s ramp from the area occupied by the 53rd TFS's F-15Cs, deployed from Bitburg. The jet closest to the camera (88-1692) was shot down by two SA-2s on 20 January 1991 whilst being flown by Col Dave Eberly and Maj Tom Griffith. Both men ejected and were captured (*USAF*)

Fellow WSO Al Gale added;

'As December approached the wing leadership was told of a new base at Al Kharj where we would deploy to at a later date in order to move us closer to Iraq. The wing CO, his director of operations and others did a site survey of the new base and briefed us on it. It had a huge ramp like the one at Nellis AFB but it was essentially just a big slab of concrete.

'When it became known that the war was going to start the squadron commander had a cookout. We all had some fun as we tried to relax right before the start of combat. Folks who were scheduled to fly the second night went around shaking hands with and wishing good luck to those who would go the first night. By this time the "Rocketeers" had been

Capt Jeff 'Lettuce Head' Lattice (left) and Lt Col Mike 'Slammer' Decuir (currently Air Combat Command's Director of Operations) wait for step-time and the crew van to take them to the flightline for departure from Thumrait to Al Kharj in December 1990 (*Jerry Oney via Author*)

The Personal Equipment area in Oman. Everything was divided up into rooms within the squadron area through the use of plywood (*Jerry Oney via Author*)

The only lieutenant pilot to deploy with the 336th TFS to Oman as part of *Desert Shield*, Steve Kwast had also been the first lieutenant pilot to graduate from training straight into the Strike Eagle programme. He is seen here during *Desert Storm* shortly after becoming a captain (*Steve Kwast via Author*)

deployed and away from home for five months. We were ready to get it over with'.

OPERATION *DESERT STORM*

On 17 January 1991, the order for the first strikes was given by President Bush – Operation *Desert Storm* had begun. With great media attention focused on Baghdad, waves of British Tornado GR 1s and American F-111Fs, F-15Cs, F-15Es, EF-111s, F-16s, F/A-18s, F-14s, A-6s, A-7s, AV-8Bs, F-4Gs and B-52s flew at low level to attack the 'eyes' and 'ears' of the Iraqi military machine. The Integrated Air Defense System (IADS) was the primary target for a lot of the first sorties, with airfields, Hardened Aircraft Shelters (HAS) and aircraft also being attacked so that air superiority could be attained.

The ATO called for later strikes against Iraqi armour, C3 (Command, Control & Communications) and logistics supplies, thus paving the way for a less protracted ground war to rid Kuwait of its occupiers.

Five fixed Scud sites in western Iraq were attacked by 24 Strike Eagles on that first night of the war, the jets being divided into three-ship or four-ship packages. Each F-15E carried two external fuel tanks, twelve Mk 20 Rockeye CBUs and two AIM-9M missiles. The exception was 'Chevy' flight, which was to attack Scud sites at H2 air base with 12 Mk 82 bombs. All of the jets would ordinarily have been loaded with four AIM-9s, but that would have taken them above the 81,000-lb maximum weight limit. Although capable of carrying an awesome bomb load, the F-15E in this heavy configuration was restricted in certain flight regimes, not the least of which was a 3g turn limitation for fear of departing the jet from controlled flight.

The fixed sites were simple to strike, and 'Dodge' flight ingressed the target area at low level at 540 knots. Briefly climbing to altitude as they neared the target, the crews patch-mapped the area before descending once again to 300 ft. AWACS called several unidentified aircraft in their locality, but none came closer than 30 miles. Azimuth steering cues on the HUD were generated so the pilot could precisely position his jet for bomb release. Nearing the target, they executed the famous 'Pop' and less aggressive 'Level' deliveries and the first jet released its CBUs at 0305 hrs local time.

Attacking the Scud sites was a risky business, for each one was ringed by AAA batteries. Several jets exceeded their G limits as pilots hauled them into jinks and evasive turns to avoid seemingly impenetrable streams of flak. In the haste to avoid the threats, at least one jet came within 90 ft of flying into the ground, saved only as a result of a 7g pull prompted by the panicked screaming of the WSO who had noted his pilot's error.

'Chevy' was the only F-15E flight to attack its target – a Scud launching facility at H2 – at medium level that night. Capt Steve Kwast, flying as 'Chevy 12', vividly recalled the sight of more than 100 AAA pieces firing in unison following the impact of 'Chevy 11's' bombs;

'We took-off out of Al Kharj and flew to our tanker track – "Banana", I think it was called – and once we tanked we dropped down to low-altitude and crossed the border. As we crossed, we could see the fires burning at the observation posts and radar facilities that our Special Forces had taken out. As we flew at 500 ft, we could see in our FLIR the

This unusual photograph of the 4th TFW(P)'s ramp at Al Kharj was taken by WSO Maj Jerry Oney as his jet entered the recovering pattern for landing at the base. The F-15Es were parked at an angle on the vast ramp to avoid sharp turns when taxiing in or out of their parking spots. The heavy combat loads (81,000 lbs) typically carried in *Desert Storm* meant that sharp turns could have caused the tyres to roll off their rims (*Jerry Oney via Author*)

Armed with four 2000-lb GBU-10 Paveway II LGBs, 335th TFS jet 88-1686 waits for its next anti-Scud sortie at Al Kharj. The GBU-10 was the weapon of choice for the 'Chiefs' when Scud hunting in *Desert Storm*. A veteran of 52 missions (a total bettered only by 87-0200's 54 within the 335th) in 1991, 88-1686 again saw action over Iraq with the 335th FS during OIF in 2003 (*USAF*)

Special Forces' helicopters flying below us at 200 ft. Other than that, it was totally pitch-black outside.

'Cruising in low, we were thinking about our two plans. One would see us perform a low altitude attack, and the other a high altitude attack. Which one we chose depended on how much AAA there was out there – lots of it would make us go high, but if there was not too much then we'd stay low and try and use the element of surprise.

'AWACS called out a MiG beaming us on the far side of the target, but it didn't look like he was aware that we were here. We looked out into the distance and you could see the AAA rising like a curtain from the ground. The squadron CO, who was leading this six-ship package, said "Climb", so we all climbed up to medium altitude and each dropped our 12 Mk 82 dumb bombs. Once we were off-target, we descended and egressed at low altitude until we neared our tanker track, at which time we climbed back up and tanked.'

Kwast was the first ever Strike Eagle 'baby' – the first pilot to go straight from undergraduate pilot training to the F-15E – and the only lieutenant pilot to deploy with the 'Rocketeers' in 1990;

'Once the initial cadre of F-15E pilots had been established, they started the pipeline for guys straight out of pilot training. I was the very first lieutenant in the very first class to go to the F-15E. My class consisted of captains – older officers with time as instructors in other jets like T-38s.

'The "experienced" guys flew all the sorties on the first two days of the war. "Experienced" was a relative term in those days, as with a few exceptions, the "experienced" guys had maybe 200 hours of F-15E time. By today's standards, they wouldn't even qualify to be flight leads, but back then the whole F-15E community was brand new. However, nearly everyone had several hundred flying hours in the F-4, or some other aircraft, so they did have a clue'.

Capt Bill 'Shadow' Schaal straps in for a mission a short while before engine start. Note the 336th TFS-marked CFT on the maintenance dolly to the left of Schaal's jet. Jerry Oney told the author that the 'maintainers and weapons guys did a wonderful job keeping us in the air in perfectly performing jets. Guys had their own habits when it came to depositing helmet bags and helmets as they strapped in. Bill hung his bag over the side, while I put mine on the instrument shield in front of the "sissy bar", which we used to help us "check-six"' *(Jerry Oney via Author)*

Downwind at Al Kharj. Jerry Oney again, 'You can see tent-city in the upper right. We were parked in the right rectangular shaped bit of concrete and the F-16s were on the left rectangular shaped parking pad. The F-15Cs from Bitburg were parked in front of us. Although tough to see, our squadron tents are just visible next to our parking area' *(Jerry Oney via Author)*

Al Gale provided the following recollection of his first night, flying in the same package as Kwast but against a different target set;

'On the first night of the war there were 21 F-15Es that went into Iraq. The original plan was for 18, but three more were added near the start time. During the mission briefing, our particular three-ship was looking at our target photos. Our targets were fixed Scud sites in western Iraq. As we looked at the target photos, there was some concern as to whether the launcher array would be oriented as in the images, so we decided to use an air-to-air type of targeting arrangement – Lead would bomb the target on the right, No 2 (us) would do the one in the middle and No 3 would take the one on the left.

'After take-off, we climbed out and avoided doing some of the usual weapons checks due to the fact that we were a big 21-ship gaggle. In the process, my pilot forgot to dial up the tone volume on his AIM-9. This would be an issue later. When we got up to the tankers, they all had their lights turned off except for one small bulb – it was a moonless night, so air refuelling was very difficult. One of the wingmen went "lost wingman" as he lost sight of the formation, but he regained his position later.

'Once the refuelling was completed, we headed north and descended to low level. We also had our lights off. Our three-ship was Nos 16-18 in the long chain of Strike Eagles heading towards their targets. We were all on the TFR at 200 ft in radio silence – the pilots were hand-flying the TFR steering while concentrating on the FLIR picture in the HUD and maintaining their formation position. The WSOs were monitoring the TFR e-scope and the radar whilst keeping the Nav systems updated. The only talking on radio was by the AWACS, who was doing a very good job providing bull's-eye locations for four groups of enemy fighters, but we didn't encounter any of these on the way in.

'When I mapped one of the update points, which was the corner of a building, it turned out that the building was rubble. As we ingressed

further we flew by it, and the building was on fire! It turned out that our update point was one of the targets taken out by US Army Apache attack helicopters tasked with paving the way for us.

'As we flew along at 0300 hrs or so (our time on target was 0308 hrs), we would occasionally pass over cars travelling on the highway. It looked just like any highway at night. It felt strange to know that those drivers, who must have heard us going by at over 500 knots, were just motoring along watching jets that were about to expend more than 200 bombs on their military. As we approached the target we took our radar map, and when it displayed, the target area looked just like it had in the pictures during the briefing. I therefore designated the Scud in the middle'.

'We climbed to 500 ft for the delivery and pushed it up to 550 knots. Given our speed, we weren't able to turn to do a "direct to the target" laser lock up and stay inside the TFR bank angle limits (the low bank angle limits made us arc the target rather than head towards it), so my pilot, Rich Crandall, pulled the nose up to ensure ground clearance and made a hard right turn to head directly to the target. We rolled out and descended back to 500 ft for the delivery.

'I was watching out for threats now, and I saw AAA start up off to our left. I mentioned it to Rich, who was concentrating on the target. The AAA looked like small stuff not too far away, but it was actually big stuff 12 miles away at H2, for the lead elements of our 21-ship group were now also over their targets.

'Rich wasn't able to confirm the target in the FLIR, so he undesignated it and bombed another Scud which was visible a little farther along. In the debrief, the big TV screen showed a better picture than in the jet, and it turned out that the designation was fine on the original target, so I didn't feel bad. It was standard procedure for the pilot to visually confirm that the designation was on the target before releasing. Anyway, our No 3 said both Nos 1 and 2 got secondary explosions from their bombs, so we were sure we had taken out a Scud like we were tasked to do.'

DAYLIGHT STRIKES

In the daylight deliveries which followed, the Dive Toss technique was used to put bombs on target from the relative sanctuary of medium level. Rolling the jet inverted from 30,000 ft and diving towards the aim point for final visual verification, the pilot would pull out no lower than 15,000 ft – the approximate ceiling for the majority of the Iraqi AAA. When the target was not accurately designated, the pilot slewed the

Top and above
Jerry Oney took these photographs during *Desert Storm*, explaining to the author that 'The first shot shows my jet sat on the ramp loaded up with 12 Mk 82s. In the second one, a section of aircraft are in the arming area having the arming pins removed from their bombs and missiles just prior to departing Al Kharj – you can just make out the armourers beneath the jets, pulling out the arming pins'. The Mk 82 500-lb bomb was unguided, forcing the F-15E crew to make the most of their jet's sophisticated computers to ensure that their weapons hit the target. Only later in the war did the much-appreciated AAQ-14 targeting pod arrive, allowing the 'Chiefs' and 'Rocketeers' to laser-guide 500-lb bombs onto their targets with much greater accuracy
(*Jerry Oney via Author*)

Target Diamond in his HUD over the correct aim point before hitting the pickle (bomb release) button.

Schaal and Oney flew their first two missions during the daytime, which was a little disconcerting as the latter explained;

'I sort of liked the advantage the night gave us, so I wasn't thrilled about flying during the day. About the funniest thing that happened in the first mission was Bill saw a guy heading west pulling a boat down one of the major highways in Iraq. We both got a good chuckle out of that one before we slung our CEM (Combined-Effects Munition, in this case CBU-87s) at some Scuds that Intel had previously located for us. I didn't see much of anything in the way of either air-air or air-ground threats during our ingress or egress, but I can tell you we had the radar working overtime, and "checking-six" wasn't just a casual pastime.

'We were sent after some more mobile Scuds on our second mission, and this was probably our most eventful one. Our two-ship had been scheduled to attack a pre-planned target, but just before step-time we got re-tasked to go after some mobile Scuds. Apparently, a section of A-10s had been looking for these things when they had bingo'd out and gone home, so we were sent to have a look. The Scuds were supposed to be located along a road in southeastern Iraq, so we pressed up there as quickly as we could.

'We crossed the border, went to a trail formation and started to look for the bad guys. In the process of looking for the Scuds, we'd found a smallish Iraqi AAA site/encampment and had patch-mapped it for future use. Personally, I wanted to sling at least one Mk 82 on the camp, but we had other priorities at the time.

'Well, there we were, a couple of the USAF's finest, flying the mighty Strike Eagle at around 2000 ft below a mostly scattered cloud deck in a two-mile trail at 500 kts conducting a road-recce for some Scuds. Even then I was thinking "this isn't the greatest idea in the history of earth". I was soon proved correct as we flew past this Iraqi airfield and saw the smoke trail of an SA-7, or maybe an SA-9, heading past us and right towards lead.

'As luck would have it, lead had just looked over his right shoulder starting an easy right turn, and he saw the missile smoke trail heading his way. The next bit of action that happened seemed compressed into about two seconds or less – lead broke hard into the missile in an attempt to defeat it, I watched the thing overshoot and detonate about 500 ft above lead (I could have sworn I actually heard the thing explode), Bill manoeuvred hard to avoid lead as we now had a *big* face-full of F-15E heading more or less right towards us. Damn, an Eagle can turn!

'I felt all of our ordnance and fuel tanks come off the aeroplane as Bill calmly punched the Jettison button as part of our attempt to avoid hitting lead and to get our weight down in anticipation of another shot coming our way. We continued our evasive action more or less to the north, and lead continued his hard manoeuvring, heading south. We eventually joined up a few minutes later – the APG-70 radar is a wonderful thing. Thank you, Hughes!

'Our day wasn't done yet though. We regrouped, got our noses in the same direction, got back into a trail formation, got down low, got real fast and headed home. Murphy's law is alive and well no matter the country or continent. We managed to fly right past that same AAA site I'd wanted to bomb not ten minutes earlier! As we came upon it, I could actually see this guy run to his quad-barrelled 23 mm gun, swing the thing around and begin shooting at us – at least this is how my mind's eye recalled it once we'd crossed back into Saudi territory.

'Well, in that particular space of time the longest distance in the world was between my brain and my mouth. I wanted to tell Bill all about the guy running to his gun, it turning towards us and about all the tracers heading our way. The net result of all those efforts was me taking the throttles and slamming them into full afterburner to help the situation out. Unbeknownst to me, Bill had seen the entire thing too, and having the throttles flung from his hands with a resounding "bang" against the stops, thought we'd been hit!

'After we figured out that we both had the same situational awareness, Bill's comment was classic, and shows what an always-thinking fighter pilot he was – and is – "that's a good way to soak up a heater!" Roger that. As an Air Force brat, I'd grown up around a lot of World War 2, Korea, and Vietnam combat aviators. One told me the story of how, unlike everyone else he'd heard on the radio after they got hit with a SAM and/or AAA, that he'd be calm and collected should he ever take rounds in his aeroplane. When that finally happened, he confessed his voice did indeed go up a few octaves. Well, during this AAA event, I'm actually replaying his story in my head before telling lead we're taking AAA (probably a wasted radio call anyway), so I reckon I'll sound cool and calm over the radio! To say I didn't sound like a play-by-play sports announcer hardly does it justice, and lead let me know just that.

'Once we got back across the border and climbed up to altitude, we both had a good belly-laugh at the whole thing.'

Unbeknownst to the TACC at the time, the Iraqis were hiding mobile Scuds in specially adapted buses and underneath road bridges. They were inventive and highly skilled in the art of deception and camouflage.

As a counter to this, the US Army/Air Force-funded state-of-the-art two protoype E-8 J-STARS (Joint Surveillance Target Attack Radar System) had prematurely finished their own Operational Test & Evaluation programme and been rushed to the region. They carried a massive Norden side-looking radar in a canoe shaped fairing beneath the lower forward fuselage, and when this was used in Synthetic Aperture Radar (SAR) mode it could detect and locate stationary objects such as parked armour or Scud launchers. By alternating the SAR mode with the Doppler Ground Moving Target mode, the radar could accurately plot slow-moving objects many miles into Iraq and Kuwait, displaying the overall tactical picture on screens manned by operators in the E-8.

TACC assigned F-15Es and A-10s to work 'Scud boxes' (patches of desert where Scud launches might be possible) every night with the E-8. If a suspected Scud was picked up on radar, the E-8 would pass the coordinates and the striker would put bombs on the target. F-15Es patrolled their Scud box for four to six hours, after which they would be relieved by another flight and sent to drop their ordnance on secondary targets – anything from armour, artillery pieces or known fixed Scud sites.

Throughout the war, the F-15E was continually frustrated by the elusive search for Scuds. Diverted from its deep strike role, it failed to have

Humour has always been a good antidote to the stresses that exist in any combat environment, and the crews of the 4th TFW(P) at Al Kharj certainly enjoyed a laugh, as this photo proves. Jerry Oney (right) models an infamous *WE ARE HUNG* t-shirt with his pilot, Bill Schaal, 'strictly for publicity purposes, don't ya know! A close friend of mine from my Jump ALO days with the 2nd Ranger Battalion had sent me some t-shirts with a request for some shots to show the folks back home. Well, Bill and I had our crew chief take some shots for us. Apparently, our wing CO, Col Hal Hornburg, heard about the photos and, thankfully, went storming over to our sister-squadron, the 335th, to find out who in the hell was wearing them!' (*Jerry Oney via Author*)

A personalised GBU-10 affixed to a CFT pylon on a 335th TFS jet (*USAF*)

much of an impact on continued Scud launches. Despite random bomb releases in the hope of dissuading the Iraqis from setting up for a launch, many of the kills claimed during the war were discredited following a more thorough, post-war analysis. This did not betray any dishonesty by the F-15E crews, but was instead indicative of the fact that they could not adequately identify what they were hitting from medium altitudes at night, even when they had the benefit of an AAQ-14 TP.

IADS

SA-2 SAM sites were dotted around Iraqi targets, and despite the largely successful SEAD effort to disable them, several remained active throughout the war. Although some SAM 'spikes' were observed on the Strike Eagle's radar warning gear, many aircrew reported that missiles were launched ballistically at them without electronic indications.

During the course of the air war, the Strike Eagle was, however, tracked by Iraqi Air Force (IrAF) MiG-23s and MiG-29s. The jet's Tactical Electronic Warfare Set provided timely warnings of these threats, and in most instances the Strike Eagles descended to low-level where radar ground clutter, in conjunction with chaff and jamming activities, offered added protection.

There were at least two notable opportunities for the Strike Eagle to claim its first kill. 'Firebird' flight was egressing its target on the opening night of the war when they picked up a contact 25 miles out and slightly to the right. It was soon identified as a MiG-29, and when it closed within range the crew attempted to engage it. They experienced difficulties in getting a good lock from their AIM-9, which was struggling to acquire the MiG-29's thermal signature, but the Sidewinder was eventually fired. Unfortunately, the weapon missed. Several other aircraft in 'Firebird' flight also attempted to engage the lone MiG-29, but errors and bad luck prevented them from downing it. Al Gale's recollection of his egress from the first mission of the war certainly fits this picture;

'We turned back to the south now and began the egress. Since we had been at the end of the chain going in we were now at the front of the chain going out. With all the AAA starting up, it was now obvious that the war had started and everybody knew it. No 1 picked up a bogey on the radar and I slewed my coverage to its position. I was soon locked onto it too. As it approached we decided it was an enemy fighter, so No 1 launched an AIM-9 at it, but this missed.

'Now the bandit was passing off our right side, so, without saying a word, Rich pulled the jet into a hard climbing right turn which set off the over-g warning system, and while "Bitching Betty" was going off, I was more worried about us hitting the ground than anything else. I had been concentrating on the e-scope and radar, but now switched to the HUD repeater display so I could see what Rich was looking at – he was

Although several F-15E crews had the opportunity to down IrAF MiG-29s in the early stages of *Desert Storm*, none were actually destroyed by the 4th TFW(P) (*USAF*)

going after the bandit and wasn't talking. Rich closed on the MiG but hesitated to shoot as he was unsure of where our No 1 was and he didn't have a good tone on the missile. We got to within minimum ranged for our AIM-9 and broke off the attack.

'It was too bad that he and I weren't thinking alike, because I had an AIM-9 tone – remember that he had left his tone volume down. If he had said "I don't have a tone", I would have said "I do", and he would have launched the missile. We were also close enough to use the gun, but I was still thinking, "don't hit the ground". If there is anything in my 26-year career that I wish I could do over, it would have been to simply say "Go for guns"! If I had, he would have, and we'd have gunned down a MiG. But instead of heroes, we were zeros. That was the only chance we ever had of getting a MiG kill.

'In the immediate aftermath of this near-kill, a missile of unknown origin was loosed off in the local area. No 3 almost hit the ground diving away from it, and shortly after that I saw a fireball as an aircraft hit the ground. You could tell it was an aeroplane because the explosion made a splash. I told Rich "somebody just hit the ground", and I was wondering whether it was one of us or one of them. Later, one of the trailing Eagles – Steve Kwast – said he had had a MiG doing a conversion turn to get behind him, and it looked like its pilot hit the ground in the turn. Steve had gone down to 100 ft on his TFR, and it was his jet that I'd likely seen.'

'Chevy' flight also missed an opportunity as their MiG-29 target turned into a fireball way off in the distance – this was later attributed to the 'Fulcrum' pilot being shot down by his own wingman. In a second example of an opportunity missed, a MiG-29 flew gently into view on the AAQ-13's FLIR image during another egress, the pilot electing not to shoot as he was uncertain that the aircraft was a MiG-29 – F-14s were due in the area within minutes, and he did not want to down a 'friendly'.

For most of the war the F-15E community focused on 'putting iron on target', but as crews gained confidence, their attitude towards MiGs changed too. Steve Kwast recalled:

'It depended on the flight lead's philosophy. There were lots of guys who'd brief, "If we see a MiG out there we are going to turn 'cold' and put it on the edge of the radar scope so that we can run around it. We'll call AWACS for an intercept and we'll stay away. If it follows us we'll turn back home and avoid an engagement – there's no need for us to engage them while we have F-15Cs out there".

The IrAF's 50-strong MiG-29 'Fulcrum' force represented the greatest overall threat to Coalition aircraft in *Desert Storm*, particularly once they had closed to within visual range. Equipped with a passive infrared acquisition system, the 'Fulcrum' had the ability – on paper, at least – to covertly acquire and attack F-15Es as they entered or departed the target area (*US DoD via Tom Cooper*)

'There were others who were more aggressive, and would brief more along the lines of, "If we see a MiG we'll try and skirt around him if he doesn't see us, but if he sees us we'll climb and kill him, and then we'll move to the target". A few were "full-on", stating "I don't care if he sees us or not – if he's in our way we'll commit, hunt him down and kill him". In the first few weeks the 'community standard' was to go around them if they did not see us – leadership allowed us to make our own tactical decisions in this

respect. Later on in the war we moved to a more aggressive stance and adopted the attitude that if we killed the MiGs on the way into the target then we wouldn't have to deal with him on the way out.'

The attitude of the Flight Lead therefore determined stores configurations, and several aircrew elected to carry AIM-7 Sparrows on one CFT in anticipation of coming up against the IrAF's MiGs. Sorties flying deep into Iraq would also promote AIM-7 carriage, as these missions generally left the F-15Es without adequate protection – the F-15Cs lacked the range to accompany the E-models over Baghdad, typically peeling away and heading home 40 miles short of the target.

On 18 January the 4th TFW(P) lost its first jet to hostile fire. Maj Donnie 'Chief Dimpled Balls' Holland (WSO) and Maj Thomas F 'Teek' Koritz were part of a six-ship strike against a Petrol Oil and Lubricant (POL) plant near Basrah, defended by SA-3, SA-6, SA-8 and Roland SAMs, in addition to a full range of radar-directed AAA. Two other F-15E packages joined 'T-Bird' flight en route that night, making for a total package of 16 jets.

'T-Bird' flight separated to ingress the target at 300 ft, intending to loft its Mk 82 bombs into the plant – a technique suitable for a large, highly explosive target such as this. Intense fire greeted them and several jets were forced to turn tail and attempt another run at the target. Koritz and Holland were 'T-Bird 16' (F-15E 88-1689), which was the sixth jet to attack the POL target. Al Gale recalled;

'The crews that returned from the Basrah POL strike described it as one of the most difficult and dangerous missions of the war. Early on in the conflict the Iraqis had all their ammo and AAA sites ready. The mission ingressed at low altitude (at night) using TFR and FLIR in the LANTIRN pods. In those days this system was flown entirely manually by the pilot. The TFR provided pitch steering to maintain you at the altitude you specified, but there was no coupling with the autopilot as there is today. The pilot had to hand fly to keep the velocity vector inside the pitch steering box. This required total concentration.

'Carrying Mk 82 bombs, "T-bird" flight intended to use loft deliveries. Ask any pilot or crew that has done a night, manual TFR loft recovery and they will tell you that it is dangerous even on a peacetime training mission. You start at low altitude and pull the nose up to your loft angle for bomb release. After release you over-bank and pull away from the target while starting your descent back to low altitude. At night, this is entirely an instrument procedure as you have no ground references to look at. The FLIR provides a black and white picture in the HUD, but there is little depth perception from it. You have to watch your altitude, bank angle and dive angle carefully. If you get outside the parameters for the TFR, you can hit the ground before it can time back in and provide pitch steering.

'Returning crews described the AAA as so intense that the tracers were lighting up the sky enough to illuminate the low-altitude aircraft. The crews were concerned that the gunners would actually be able to see them due to the amount of light from the tracers flying over the top of the aircraft. They said it was like flying through a tunnel of AAA. The mission was successful and the fires from the exploding POL storage area made for even more illumination.

'One of the returning crews said they saw Tom and Donnie in a steep climb from the loft manoeuvre, so they had successfully delivered their bombs. But later still, a crew saw a fireball on the ground which was apparently from their jet. As far as I know, nobody ever knew whether or not they were shot down or if they just hit the ground during their loft recovery manoeuvre. Ultimately, it doesn't matter – after the war the Iraqis returned their bodies and we held a memorial service for them back in Goldsboro, North Carolina.'

Two nights later came the second, and final, F-15E loss. Flying in 88-1692, Col David Eberly and Maj Thomas E Griffith Jr were downed by an SA-2 on 20 January while attacking a fixed Scud site. They ejected and managed to evade capture for several days, Eberly making contact with two Coalition aircraft as he attempted to arrange a rescue. Back in the TACC, Mike Smyth rushed to arrange for Search and Rescue (SAR) crews to go and pick the crew up, but he was met with the battling egos of SAR specialists and the Special Forces teams, who refused to cooperate lest one take credit for a successful rescue over the other!

Smyth was also hindered by security issues. Despite tapes of Eberly's transmissions being recorded and played to Gen Charles Horner, Commander, US Central Command Air Forces, the latter refused to allow a rescue until Eberly had identified himself using the correct codes. Later that evening an intelligence officer showed Smyth satellite imagery of what he believed was a rescue signal made by one of the downed flyers. When Smyth could not determine the symbol to be a rescue marker, he asked the officer how he had come to this conclusion. He was told that greater resolution imagery was available but he was not cleared to see it!

With SAR forces arguing amongst themselves, Horner refusing to delay a pre-planned CBU drop in the area until Eberly authenticated himself and Intelligence refusing to allow him to see imagery which might prove conclusively that Eberly and Griffith were signalling for a rescue, Smyth was left virtually impotent to help.

The downed crewmen were subsequently captured following several days of evasion and duly paraded on television as war trophies. The entire episode dented the confidence of the 4th TFW(P) in the integrity of the Joint Rescue Coordination Centre, but also uplifted their spirits as they knew that their two colleagues were still alive. Lt Col Klett reflected;

'I sat at the duty desk and answered phones for the most part. On the first two nights of the war I took group photos of almost all the guys as they stepped to the jets. I later realised that I took the last photo of Donnie Holland who was killed near Basra along with his pilot, Maj Koritz. A sergeant in the squadron would pick me up in tent city every day and drive me over to the squadron to sit at the duty desk and answer the telephone. Two days in a row he greeted with the bad news that we had lost a jet the night before. Two crews lost in the first four or five days was fairly sobering, although the fact that the overall Coalition force loss rate was surprisingly small helped us to remain positive.'

TYPICAL SORTIES

Within a few days the flow of the sorties was beginning to become routine, although there remained many who, like Gary Klett, had yet to fly their first sortie;

'To say that I was fairly keyed up on the night of my first combat sortie would be an understatement. My target was a mobile SA-6 launcher located just south of the runway at Tallil air base in southeast Iraq. That's it. No target photo, no accurate coordinates, just a word picture. Great. I was flying with one of the other "MQ Maggots", Al "Herr Pie" Pierson. He had flown two combat sorties in the week prior. I ended up crewed with him for most of the war.

Two of the 335th TFS F-15Es in this shot carry light grey tanks raided from F-15C units at Al Kharj due to a shortage of drop tanks (*USAF***)**

336th TFS jets bask in the sunshine at Al Kharj between missions (*USAF***)**

'We made a good team. We briefed up the sortie and off we went. Since it was a close target, we didn't have to air refuel, so it was fairly uneventful on the trip north. I spent the whole time finding things with the radar and running through the process to designate them as targets. I wanted to make sure I didn't dork up my first attack due to some dumb-ass switch error. Map, update, target, map, update, target. I must have done it 50 times in as many minutes.

'We had six aeroplanes in two- to four-mile trail position, and we were number six. There were other flights hitting targets in the area, so the AAA was already active and visible before we crossed the border. Almost all of it was small calibre and wasn't reaching up to our altitude, but there were a few intermittent bursts. At 20 miles from the target we checked left about 45 degrees in order to map it with the radars.

'I could see the runway very clearly and a few dots south of the middle of the runway, but I couldn't guarantee that any of them was the SA-6 launcher. Again, great. So, I just picked a dot with a few other

dots clustered around it and designated it as the target. I could also plainly see the security fence that surrounded the whole complex. I always wanted to thank Saddam for putting those around most sites of military value. They showed up like radar reflectors in the desert, making it very easy to ensure we weren't bombing civilian areas.

'We rolled into a 30-degree dive about five miles from the target and then waited for the computer to decide when to release the bombs. All the pilot had to do was keep the velocity vector symbol on the steering line and hold the pickle button down. The computer decided when to release the bombs in order to hit the target. We didn't have a LANTIRN TP on our jet so we were loaded with 12 Mk 82 500-lb bombs. The jet rattled around fairly well when 6000 lbs of iron got dumped overboard in about two seconds. We pulled out of the dive and I found our element lead in the radar and pointed him out to "Herr Pie". He could see him in the HUD since we did have a LANTIRN Navigation Pod, which displayed an IR view of the world.

'As we ran out of the target area like proverbial scalded-ass apes, I finally had a few spare moments to actually look around and see the AAA popping. Nothing was very close to us, so it was more interesting than scary. On the ingress to the target I was too busy, and scared of dorking something up, to be worried about getting hit. They say dumb animals are not frightened of distant flashing lights, and I guess I resembled that remark! We could see the flashes of the bombs detonating, but we still couldn't tell if we had actually hit anything worthwhile. Some stuff was burning as we left. Since nobody could prove differently, we claimed a successful hit on the enemy dots. Some satellite photo analyst would have to decide if our ex-dots were once an SA-6!

'When we got back we celebrated my "cherry" combat sortie with a couple of shots from a highly illegal Jack Daniels bottle. All of the "MQ Maggots" eventually ended up getting credit for a tactical check ride following our first combat sortie. We even got the standard "Form 8" that normally gets filled out by the evaluator after a check ride. That officially made us mission qualified – and we probably still hold the record for the shortest MQT programme in F-15E history.'

Jerry Oney recounted his first night mission on Day Three of the war;

'Our first night mission was a bit of an "E-Ticket ride". For those not old enough to remember, E-Tickets were used on Disneyland's best rides, and you only got a couple in each book of tickets. On this particular sortie we were "Blue 16" – the last F-15E in a long, strung-out train of 16 jets. I think our call-sign that night was "Buick". We were supposed to attack a fertiliser (read chemical) plant up near Al Qa'im, on Iraq's northwestern border with Syria near the Euphrates River.

'We had a full-up package that night with F-15Cs out in front for air-air escort along with some F-4Gs for SAM suppression. The Wild Weasels shot some HARM at several SAM sites, and we heard

The AAQ-13 Navigation Pod (below) provided an infrared (IR) image to the crew of the terrain ahead, and also offered a terrain following capability for low-level flight. The AAQ-14 Targeting Pod (bottom) sat opposite the Navigation Pod and featured a laser rangefinder and IR sensor with which to acquire and target objects of interest (*FJPhotography.com*)

them on the radio working those targets too. The guys near the front of the package remarked later that they saw some SAMs launched, with the doughnut-shaped smoke ring around the launch sites.

'There was enough moonlight out and the visibility was good enough that Bill and I could see most of what was going on way up ahead of us. This included tons and tons of AAA, and we even thought we saw some B-52s way out in front and up above our altitude dropping their mega-loads of Mk 82s crossing from left to right. We asked about that later, and it turned out that the "BUFFs" were actually up there that night. This also happened to be the same place that one of our guys had been shot down the night before.

'All of this is running around in my head – the AAA show going on out front, last night's shoot down, the Wild Weasels working the SAMs – when I realise my right leg is shaking ever so slightly. I was about to ask Bill to turn up the heat when I realised my leg wasn't shaking because I was cold! Well, I quickly tucked that bit of awareness away and went back to work.

'Bill was great about moving the jet around so we could "check six" easily and, at least in my mind, our crew-coordination was mostly via extra-sensory perception – not much had to be said between us. We kept the radar in the air-air mode looking for threats and plotting AWACS bull's-eye calls until we were around 25 miles from the target.

'When Bill checked left I told him I was "heads down" and then went to the air-ground mode to take a patch-map of the target area. The APG-70 couldn't patch map head-on to the target, so we turned left or right as the target/threats dictated to take a targeting map. The target itself was pretty big, but we used a bridge as an offset aim point just to make sure, and we had worked with our Intel buddies to confirm both aim point and target coordinates during mission planning.

'Once the targeting was all squared away, my job was to go back to "checking six" for threats. Just before we rolled in on the target from 18,000 ft, and with me straining my neck to the right side looking for anything, I heard Bill say, "Man, I can't believe I'm doing this".

'As you might imagine, curiosity got the cat, so the "checking of our six" stopped and I looked around just as we were starting downhill towards the target. I tell you what, I didn't know things could get that bright from the amount of AAA being tossed up at us – it was everywhere. Just like flying into the middle of a 4th of July fireworks display. I decided right then to go back to looking behind us, because if one can't see what's being shot at you, it doesn't therefore exist!

'To make this "E-Ticket ride" even yet more interesting, for some damn software reason our pickle altitude of around 10,000 ft didn't happen! We were smoking downhill at around 480 knots, waiting for this load of 12 Mk 82s to come off the jet, with Bill following the computer's steering commands just so, and still waiting for these computer-released bombs to be computer-released just so! We were about to come off dry when the "clunk-clunk-clunk" of everything being released was both heard and felt. We were already in the air-air mode, so we found our lead, joined up and headed home.

'Crossing the border, I handed Bill a soda and popped my own in what became a bit of a mission tradition for us. After we landed and were taxiing back in, a bunch of the maintenance guys, God bless them, had lined up and were doing the "Wave" as we taxied by. Thanks, fellas!'

POD SHORTAGES AND AN AIR-TO-AIR KILL

For much of *Desert Storm*, the 4th TFW(P) operated without the AAQ-14 TP. Those pods that did arrive were quickly rushed into service, and when used would often only be carried by the lead jet of a particular package. In instances where an additional pod was available, this was usually assigned to the element lead (No 3 in a formation of four). The pod was immeasurably useful at night, and was therefore mostly used by the 335th TFS, which had finally been given the order to deploy. The 'Chiefs' received the pods because of its Scud hunting role and its responsibility for flying the night schedule.

The 'Chiefs' flew almost two weeks of solid Scud kill box missions, always using the TP, not only because it helped them to identify these elusive targets from medium altitude at night, but also because it offered some form of bomb damage assessment capability – a function which had hampered crews when they came to provide a realistic estimate of the level of damage they had inflicted on their target.

Following what amounted to a monopoly on the 16 TPs that were in theatre by the end of January, the 'Chiefs' finally passed a few examples to the 'Rocketeers'. The 336th TFS used them to drop a limited number of LGBs on high value targets such as airfields and bridges, and the unit also augmented the 'Chiefs' on Scud hunting sorties. When necessary, the two squadrons worked with each other to buddy-lase LGBs onto the target – a job at which the TP excelled. On one memorable sortie, four F-15Es equipped with AAQ-14s destroyed 18 IrAF jets at Tallil air base using CBU-87s and GBU-12 LGBs. 'Tank plinking' was another successful area for TP-equipped F-15Es, and was a term borrowed from the F-111F community. It was a politically incorrect euphemism for lasing GBU-12s onto semi-buried Iraqi armour, and was akin to shooting fish in a barrel.

On 14 February 1991 the F-15E scored its first, and only, air-to-air kill – a Mil Mi-24 'Hind' attack helicopter. In response to a request for help from US Special Forces, AWACS called the F-15E (89-0487) manned by Capts Richard T Bennett and Dan B Bakke to ask for assistance. Arming and selecting a single GBU-10 LGB, Bennett took the F-15E at full power through bad weather and into the area as directed. At 50 miles out, Bakke picked up contacts on the radar and later cued the TP as they broke through the weather at 3000 ft.

They closed the last 20 miles as Iraqi AAA crews fired their weapons towards where they thought the F-15E was – a technique Strike Eagle aircrew came to call derisively 'sound-activated AAA'. Two of three helicopters closing on the Special Forces squad were now clearly visible through the TP, so Bakke pickled the GBU-10 six miles from the target – it would have a 30-second time of flight to reach the 'Hind'.

As the 30 seconds came and went, the crew assumed that the bomb had missed or failed to detonate. Bennett pulled the jet into a left turn, his intention being to come back and target the helicopters with an AIM-9 or two. But as they reefed the jet around again, the 'Hind' blew up and literally vapourised. Special Forces troops on the ground nearby estimated that the helicopter was at a height of about 800 ft when the bomb impacted just in front of the main rotor. The call '"Cougar" (AWACS), "Packard 41" (F-15E) splash one helicopter' was made.

Bakke and Bennett continued to target the second 'Hind', but despite acquiring it on radar, fuel considerations, and a real concern that they might hit a friendly Special Forces helicopter, forced them to return to base. The pair had just made history, but it would not be officially recognised until 2 November 2001, when the USAF painted a green kill marking on 89-0487 at a ceremony attended by Bennett and Bakke.

Following 42 days of intensive combat flying, a cease-fire came into effect at midnight on 1 March 1991. Northern and Southern no-fly zones were quickly established in Iraq to prevent IrAF fixed-wing aircraft from posing a threat to the Coalition. Despite this, Saddam Hussein made full use of a loop hole that allowed helicopters to operate in the No-Fly Zones, and ordered Mi-24s to strike Kurdish refugees in northern Iraq. Helpless and unable to offer protection, F-15E crews enforcing the No-Fly Zone watched in horror as the gunships started attacking 600 civilians in the village of Chamchamal as they fled towards Turkey.

The modest bomb tally carried on the 336th TFS F-15E assigned to Lt Col Mike 'Slammer' Decuir and his WSO, Maj Tom Griffith. The latter was shot down on 20 January 1991 while flying with Col David Eberly in F-15E 88-1692. Captured several days later, both crewmen were released by their Iraqi captors on 4 March 1991. The 336th flew 1100 sorties, logged 3200 flying hours and dropped 6.5 million pounds of ordnance in *Desert Storm* (*USAF*)

The 335th TFS's CO jet leads a 336th TFS F-15E and an F-15C from the 53rd TFS over a devastated airfield in Kuwait shortly after the end of the war. The 'Chiefs' flew 1097 combat missions and dropped 4.8 million pounds of ordnance during *Desert Storm* (*USAF*)

Left middle and bottom
Jerry Oney took these photographs of the 'Rocketeers' during the unit's return trip to Seymour Johnson after *Desert Storm* had ended. The bottom shot shows the jets on the ground at Zaragosa, in Spain. 'We took off from Saudi Arabia and flew to Zaragosa, where we spent the night, and then departed the following day for North Carolina. I had stowed a can of Coke with Arabic writing all over it in the cockpit to take home as a souvenir, and when I came out to the jet the next day our crew chief – Sgt Dennis Bagley – had just finished drinking it!' In the top photo, F-15Es receive fuel from a 305th Air Refueling Wing KC-135R in northern Saudi Arabia (*Jerry Oney via Author*)

Denied the ability to fire upon the Iraqis, the F-15E crews made high speed passes as close as they dared in the hope that their wake turbulence would snap a rotor blade. They also fired their lasers into the cockpit of the 'Hinds' with the intention of blinding the pilots. Whilst the latter technique was probably ineffective, the former was enough to cause the gunships to land, and in one instance caused a 'Hind' to crash. As USAF leadership became wise to these activities, they ordered that the F-15Es not fly below 10,000 ft.

Operation *Provide Comfort* was launched following the US-encouraged Kurdish uprising in the northern territories against Iraq's dictator. Saddam Hussein's response was to overpower the rebel fighters and to embark upon a policy of ethnic cleansing. Unable to stand by and watch any longer, the UN passed Security Council Resolution 688 to allow UN-sanctioned intervention. *Provide Comfort* sought the achievement of two goals – to provide relief to the refugees and to ensure the security of the refugees and the humanitarian effort assisting them.

These two goals were maintained from April to September 1991 by a US led Combined Task Force. Over 40,000 sorties were flown in support of efforts to relocate over 700,000 refugees and restore 70-80 per cent of the villages destroyed by the Iraqis. Ironically, all of this was happening while Turkey launched its own attacks with fast jets against the Kurds with complete impunity.

F-15Es were provided by the 'Chiefs' for *Provide Comfort* until July 1991, at which time *Provide Comfort II* began.

NO-FLY ZONES

Continuing on from Operations *Desert Storm* and *Provide Comfort*, the 492nd FS sent six of its newly-acquired F-15Es to Incirlik AB, in Turkey, on 2 August 1993 and flew 431 sorties prior to returning home on 2 November. The unit was replaced the following day by the 494th FS, which flew no fewer than 1413 sorties over the next three months. Based at RAF Lakenheath with the 48th FW, these two F-15E units were a direct replacement for the four squadrons of F-111Fs that had previously been based in the sleepy Suffolk town.

The 'Panthers' (494th FS) returned to Incirlik again in October 1994 and 1995, the latter deployment seeing eight jets in-country in January-February. The 'Bolars' (492nd FS) sent 12 jets to Turkey in July of that year too, conducting patrols until September. In 1996 the 492nd made its final deployment (12 jets), after which the 391st FS from Mountain Home deployed six jets for three months. The 'Bold Tigers'' deployment

F-15Es from the 48th FW's 492nd FS 'Mad Hatters' (below) and 494th FS 'Panthers' (bottom) conduct training sorties from their home base of RAF Lakenheath, in Suffolk. The 48th began replacing its F-111Fs with F-15C/Es in 1992, and that same year Tactical Air Command and Strategic Air Command were combined to form Air Combat Command, resulting in the deletion of 'Tactical' from all Air Force nomenclature. Thus, the 4th TFW became the 4th FW and the 48th TFW became the 48th FW (*FJPhotography.com*)

marked the end of *Provide Comfort II* and the beginning of Operation *Northern Watch* (ONW).

A DECADE OF OPERATIONS

Operations *Northern Watch* and *Southern Watch* (OSW) policed the northern and southern No-Fly Zones set up with the conclusion of *Desert Storm*. These zones, authorised by UN Security Council Resolutions 678, 687 and 688, existed above the 36th parallel (ONW) and below the 32nd parallel (OSW). Evolved over more than a decade, the operations moved from instant retaliatory strikes to more considered, delayed Response Options (RO) in later years. The evolution took place largely out of the public eye – indeed, many members of the public were oblivious to the fact that the US and Britain were still flying daily combat missions over Iraq – but there were notable exceptions.

The sheer volume of sorties and actions over this time exceeds the scope of even this book, but the passages below attempt to give a flavour of the evolving modus operandi, and to highlight some of the F-15E's more significant or noteworthy actions.

In January 1993 the 4th FW(P) led a small package to hit Iraqi targets that broke the rules of the ceasefire by deploying below the 32nd Parallel. The Strike Eagles specifically targeted an SA-3 Goa SAM site with success. Several days later, ten F-15Es were in the vanguard of an additional punitive strike.

On the whole, most missions flown in ONW and OSW were of a defensive nature, and the F-15Es carried a broad selection of stores to allow them to retaliate if necessary. Operating under the close supervision of AWACS, crews did sometimes receive airborne taskings and subsequently flew unplanned attacks against perpetrating ground targets. Occasionally, as with the SA-3 example above, pre-planned, punitive strikes would be flown, although these tended to be few and far between.

IrAF incursions above the 36th parallel intensified in 1993, but far more problematic was the constant harassment that Coalition fighters experienced from Iraqi SAM and AAA systems. Such harassment prompted 11 separate days' worth of Coalition responses in northern Iraq that year. Most often, reconnaissance aircraft were illuminated by fire control radars of illegally sited SAM systems. Sometimes, as in the case of two F-111Fs on 13 January, AAA pieces actually engaged the No-Fly Zone enforcers.

In most instances, retaliatory strikes were not executed, although severe breaches of the agreement did sometimes elicit an immediate response. On 17 January an F-4G attacked an air defence site that was targeting French Jaguars performing low-level reconnaissance. Some 90 minutes later an F-16 shot down an Iraqi MiG-23 over northern Iraq. These actions followed an earlier incident the same day when Iraqi AAA fired on two F-16s. Neither was hit and neither returned fire.

In the three years that followed Iraq withdrew slightly and the number of incursions and engagements reduced. UN weapons inspectors were also admitted to Iraqi installations to check for tell-tale signs of weapons of mass destruction (chemical, biological and nuclear). In 1997, Turkey approved the creation of ONW and officially allowed the use of Incirlik air base as the staging post and headquarters for US and British assets.

The creation of ONW was more of a re-branding exercise than a change in operations or tasking, as Incirlik had been the home for US and British aircraft involved in *Provide Comfort I/II* for more than six years by this point. Indeed, the base had initially been inhabited by Coalition aircraft during *Desert Storm*.

AIR EXPEDITIONARY FORCES CONCEPT

As part of an effort to modernise the US Air Force, the Air Expeditionary Forces (AEF) concept was introduced in the early 1990s in response to the increasing number of contingencies that called for worldwide deployments. At its core was the goal of planning far enough ahead so that each USAF wing could benefit from some form of predictability when it came to deployments away from home. Under AEF, almost all of the USAF was divided into ten force packages, each with a cross-section of weapon systems drawn from geographically separated units.

Typically controlling about 175 aircraft, each AEF was usually more formidable than the air forces of most nations. AEFs had to be able to respond to any unexpected contingency within 72 hours of being notified, and routine deployments usually saw squadrons deployed for 90 days every 15 months. Two AEF wings remained on-call at all times.

AEFs took the form of deployed wings, groups or squadrons attached to an Air & Space Expeditionary Task Force (ASETF) – the organisation assigned to fulfil the AEF campaign objectives. F-15E squadrons (like all others) assigned or attached to an ASETF added 'expeditionary' to the end of their unit designation when deployed (i.e. 494th FS(E)). The first application of the AEF deployment concept came in ONW and OSW, both of which ceased when OIF (see Chapter 6) began in March 2003.

In August 1997 the 391st FS 'Bold Tigers' deployed six E-models to Sheikh Isa air base, in Bahrain for OSW as part of AEF V. They flew 641 hours enforcing the No-Fly Zone before leaving in October. 'Diplomacy'

Two 494th FS F-15Es prepare to depart from Incirlik on the unit's very first ONW mission in April 1997. The squadron had flown dozens of near-identical sorties as part of *Provide Comfort I/II* in 1993-95, however. Note the HARM-toting F-16CJs of the 23rd FS/52nd FW, deployed to Turkey from Spangdahlem air base in Germany (*USAF*)

The 12 GBU-12 bomb markings below the crew name plate of this 492nd FS jet (97-0222) denote a reasonably busy time during the unit's one and only deployment (AEF IV) to OSW in March 2001. Bomb markings were usually applied in-theatre, and were not maintained once the airframes returned home. Sometimes these markings had faded to the extent that their outline could be discerned only when viewed from just the right angle. Other times, they would be removed altogether prior to the jet being resprayed with a fresh coat of paint. 97-0222 is still presently assigned to the 48th FW (*FJPhotography.com*)

The varied nature of the F-15E's contribution to the No-Fly Zone missions post-*Desert Storm* is evident from this photograph, taken by WSO Lt Col Gary Klett during a 492nd FS Incirlik *Provide Comfort II* deployment in the mid-1990s. These aircraft both carry mixed loads of two AIM-120C AMRAAMs, two AIM-9M Sidewinders, three CBU-87 CBUs and two GBU-12s for flexible taskings against both hard and soft targets (*Gary Klett via Author*)

This unusual view was also taken by Lt Col Klett on the same sortie as the photograph above, the F-15E's mixed load-out being even more evident (*Gary Klett via Author*)

ground to a halt in 1998 when Iraq refused to allow UNSCOM inspectors continued access, and from 16 to 19 December the US and Britain conducted a four-day aerial bombing campaign against key Iraqi installations, entitled Operation *Desert Fox*, by way of retaliation.

From March to June 1998 the 'Bold Tigers' deployed 12 jets to the same base as part of AEF VII. Whilst the 391st FS stayed in Bahrain for these two deployments, it would later find itself stationed at Al Jaber Air Base, in Kuwait, with ten jets for a three-month AEF deployment between January and March 1999. The unit also deployed ten jets to Incirlik later that same year as the 391st honoured its AEF commitments to ONW. 48th FW 'Liberty Wing' F-15Es also deployed for operations, the 494th FS sending six Strike Eagles to Incirlik from January to April 1997, during which time they dropped 75 tonnes of ordnance on Iraqi SAM and AAA pieces. In September the 492nd FS also deployed to Incirlik with six jets.

In December 1998 the 494th FS again returned to Turkey, and a two-ship top-up flight deployed on 15 January 1999 brought the unit's strength up to ten jets. The 'Panthers' left in February 1999 when they were replaced by ten 492nd FS jets, which were in turn relieved by a detachment of 336th FS from Seymour Johnson in April.

1999 saw the busiest period of retaliatory and pre-planned strikes in the history of ONW, with weapons being expended against Iraqi targets on no fewer than 105 separate days. The vast majority of the these raids were performed by mission packages of F-16CJs and F-15E Strike Eagles, and, more often than not, several targets were attacked on each day. The F-16CJs carried two AGM-88 HARM anti-radiation missiles for the suppression of enemy air defences (SEAD), whilst the F-15Es often sortied with mixed loads of LGBs and electro-optical or infrared stand-off GBU-15s and AGM-130s.

In one three-day period in 1999 (which had been preceded by three days of F-15E and F-16CJ strikes), US European Command reported the following incidents;

'24 January 1999. Between 1430 and 1530 hrs, Coalition aircraft were again targeted by Iraqi SAM and AAA systems near Mosul. An EA-6B Prowler and two F-16CJs fired HARMs in self-defence. The aircraft responded to being targeted by Iraqi radars that were being used to guide AAA. Another F-16CJ fired a HARM at an Iraqi SAM. Earlier in the day, an F-15E Strike Eagle scored a direct hit with an AGM-130 on an Iraqi SA-3 SAM site which posed a threat to Coalition forces in the region.

'25 January 1999. Between 1357 and 1430 hrs Iraqi time, Coalition aircraft were again illuminated and fired upon by Iraqi SAM and AAA systems in several incidents. An F-15E was fired upon by a AAA system, after which two F-15Es then dropped one GBU-12 each on the site. In another incident on this date, an EA-6B launched a HARM at an SA-2 SAM site that posed a threat to Coalition forces in the area. An F-16CJ launched a HARM at a different SA-2 SAM site that also posed a threat to Coalition forces in the area. Coalition forces observed an Iraqi SAM launch in the vicinity of Coalition aircraft, the latter duly departing the area and continuing operations elsewhere.

'26 January 1999. Between 1325 and 1350 hrs Iraqi time, Coalition aircraft were targeted by Iraqi SAM and AAA systems in three separate incidents near Mosul. An EA-6B Prowler, acting in self-defence after being targeted by Iraqi radar, launched a HARM at an Iraqi radar site. An F-15E dropped a GBU-12 500-lb LGB in response to a AAA system which posed a threat to Coalition aircraft. In another incident, two F-15Es each fired an AGM-130 at a radar site which had targeted Coalition aircraft. Finally, between 1500 and 1530 hrs local time, Coalition aircraft were again targeted by AAA systems near Mosul. Three F-15Es, acting in self-defence after being targeted by Iraqi AAA systems, dropped GBU-12s.'

The ONW/OSW mission continued to be shared between five squadrons from the 4th and 48th FWs and the 366th AEW over the next three years during regular AEF deployments to Incirlik and Al Jaber.

ROs AND THE F-15E

The F-15E was the primary tool used to implement and enforce ROs and spontaneous retaliatory strikes over Iraq for the duration of both No-Fly Zone operations. As we have seen, during the early 1990s the jet was used to prosecute many of the threatening SAM and AAA systems that took pot shots at loitering Coalition aircraft, but in the years leading up to OIF, pre-planned, RO-oriented strikes became the norm.

The F-15E squadrons were the most highly-tasked of all the USAF's tactical fighter units simply because there were fewer of them to fulfil AEF taskings. Of the six operational F-15E squadrons, three were also assigned to the emergency Air Expeditionary Wing (AEW) concept – the 335th and 336th FSs to the 4th AEW and the 391st FS to the 366th AEW. The 90th FS was permanently attached to the Pacific Air Forces' 3rd Wing, thus being exempt from AEF cycles until 2002, and the remaining two squadrons, assigned to the 48th FW (492nd and 494th FSs), carried the dual responsibility of being assets both of USAF Europe and also NATO.

The road to adopting ROs as the primary means of enforcing the OSW/ONW mission saw several different stages. Initially, immediate responses to AAA or SAM fire were replaced with delayed, punitive strikes, often flown the same day, but adhering to the adage that 'retaliation is a dish best eaten cold'.

This soon evolved into an even more considered approach, whereby the Coalition exercised the right to attack *any* Iraqi military target in the southern No-Fly Zone. It did not even have to be the one that prompted the reaction in the first place. This, in turn, finally led to the pre-planned RO methodology of recent times. Capt Randall Haskin, a Strike Eagle pilot with the 336th FS, explained that 'this philosophy was basically one where it was better to come back later with all of the appropriate assets on hand (OCA, SEAD, etc.) rather than to knee-jerk react to getting shot at and risk actually getting hit'.

ROs offered real advantages in terms of safety, precision, reducing the possibility of collateral damage and achieving the job with the minimum firepower required. Each Strike Eagle crew planned and prepared to attack its targets as it would on any other mission, so if the CAOC called for an RO to be executed whilst the package was in flight, there was a good chance that the target would be struck with precision and good effect.

The nature of these marauding strike packages led the Strike Eagle community to coin the phrase 'roving motorcycle gang' according to one F-15E pilot, who added 'we are like a group of bikers loaded with weapons looking for a fight and going no place in particular'.

The CAOC could raise an ATO that specifically called for a measured response to increasing Iraqi violations or a particularly serious misdemeanour, in which case the crew briefed for that target, and a secondary target, before launching in exactly the same way as they would have done for a normal patrol. On these occasions, however, the F-15E crews knew as they headed out of the door and stepped towards their waiting jets that this time they would definitely be dropping iron!

Strike Eagle crews principally flew three types of OSW missions – container sorties, which involved penetrating the No-Fly Zone as strikers or Defensive Counter Air fighters, scouting for IrAF aircraft; alert sorties, where crews waited for the 'Bat Phone' to ring and scramble them to investigate a target in the No-Fly Zone; and normal continuation training (CT) sorties, which allowed air-to-air practice against one another, or other aircraft. F-15E deployments were always made to either Al Jaber or Sheikh Isa because of the political implications of having strike aircraft based in Saudi Arabia. They therefore had numerous opportunities to fly, and crews typically completed at least four missions per week (2-3 combat sorties and 1-2 CT sorties).

Container sorties were usually executed by a four-ship flight of F-15Es tasked to patrol a geographically prescribed box (known in fighter-speak as a 'container'). If they spotted a violation of the No-Fly Zone they would report it and await further instructions from the CAOC, which decided whether to execute one or more of the ROs. Pilots and WSOs usually took off with imagery of three or four RO target areas onboard, although it was unusual for more than a single RO to be executed on any given sortie.

Alert sorties were, by definition, less proactive and more reactive, with aircrew remaining dressed in full flight gear (flight suit, g-suit, parachute harness and survival vest) for the duration of the 12-hour shift. Standing the alert meant a level of discomfort for crews trussed up in their flying gear for hours on end, but it was essential if they were to be strapped into their jets and ready to taxi within three minutes of receiving the call from the CAOC. Such calls typically arose when either an aircraft or ground contact required further investigation. Typical load-outs in support of

OSW included GBU-12s, GBU-10s, AGM-130s, AIM-120s and AIM-9s. The use of Rockeye CBUs was rare on account of the indiscriminate nature of the weapon.

FDL AND AIR-TO-GROUND OPS

The Iraqi military tended not to draw attention to itself, and to limit its operations to times when it stood the greatest chance of success. This meant that it was mobile, allowing it to rapidly reposition to avoid retaliatory attacks once it was detected.

Such tactics were something of a headache for the Strike Eagle until the F-15E became a recipient of Fighter Data Link (FDL) in the final year of ONW/OSW. Hurriedly installed prior to the Strike Eagles' deployment to Operation *Enduring Freedom* (OEF) in Afghanistan in October 2001 (see Chapter 5), FDL allowed the expeditious transfer of target coordinates and information between RC-135 *Rivet Joint*, E-8 J-STARS, F-15C, F-16, F-15E and E-3 AWACS platforms as soon as a target was detected.

Whilst most of the RO target-sets were fixed in nature (ammunition bunkers, command and control facilities etc.), Strike Eagles were tasked with attacking inherently mobile targets such as the towed 100 mm KS-19 AAA batteries and SA-3/6 tracked launchers before they had the opportunity to move to other locations.

In basic terms, FDL allows the F-15E crew to receive data from other sources and sensors and to piece together a top down oriented picture

A 336th FS F-15E closes on the flying boom of a KC-10A during an OSW CT sortie from Doha, in Qatar, in February 1997 (*USAF*)

This 492nd F-15E is configured for maximum flexibility, carrying two AIM-7Ms, two AIM-9Ms, two AIM-120Cs and two GBU-12s (*Gary Klett via Author*)

of the battlefield. E-8 J-STARS, RC-135 *Rivet Joint* and E-3 AWACS aircraft are able to pass precise locations of ground targets, threat emitters, hostile aircraft, other 'friendlies' and additional data via their own Link 16 terminals to the F-15E in real time. Strike Eagle crews can then call up a 'SIT' (SITuation) display on one of their Multi Purpose Displays and observe these target tracks, even if they are beyond the range of their own sensors.

To accomplish this, Link 16 uses 128 Time Division Multiple Access time slots per second to exchange information between units at up to 238 kb per second. For example, AWACS might wish to pass an airborne track report, which would route through the E-3's Link 16 terminals, onto the UHF/HF network, into the F-15E FDL box, through the Strike Eagle's Central Computer and then appear on the screen as a symbol. Collectively, jets passing data are referred to as the 'network'.

Configured exclusively for offensive counter air (OCA), a 492nd Strike Eagle patrols high over northern Iraq armed with two AIM-7Ms, two AIM-9Ms and two AIM-120Cs. It was rare to see an F-15E on an ONW/OSW patrol without LGBs bolted onto its CFT pylons. This jet has served exclusively with the 492nd FS since its delivery to the USAF in August 1992 (*Gary Klett via Author*)

FDL takes on additional functionality in the F-15E. As targets are passed to the crew, controlling authorities such as *Rivet Joint*, AWACS or J-STARS can assign 'actions' to the Strike Eagle without the need to speak over the radio. They may wish to action the destruction of a specific target, and can assign this to any F-15E logged onto the network. In this instance, the symbol representing the target will be highlighted to the crew and an option to accept or decline that tasking is then communicated back at the simple press of a push button.

Similarly, FDL allows the Strike Eagle crew to select their own target and pass information back to AWACS to state that they are attacking it. For the duration, FDL frequently sends out own-ship weapons status (how many and what type), fuel status, radar and sensor status information to the rest of the network, and receives similar information from the other network participants.

FDL therefore facilitated Time Sensitive Targeting (TST) missions, permitting the F-15E to instantly locate targets and to 'hook' radar and IR weapons guidance systems directly onto the FDL-generated target.

OSW AND ONW EXPERIENCES

'Grinder', an F-15E pilot with the 492nd FS on deployment from RAF Lakenheath to Al Jaber for AEF IV in March 2001, recalled;

'The container sorties saw us fly into Iraq as strikers or on DCA, which we didn't do very often down there, the alert sorties had you waiting for the "Bat Phone" to ring to send you on your way running to investigate someone in the No-Fly Zone and normal CT sorties had crews fighting each other, or aircraft from another unit. I had some great CT sorties down there, fighting Bahraini Vipers (F-16s), Kuwaiti, Marine and Navy F/A-18s and Navy F-14s. These were firsts for me, as I didn't have much experience fighting dissimilar aircraft. During an average week I'd fly 2-3 combat sorties and 1-2 CT sorties.

'I'll never forget my first combat sortie. "Skull" was my flight lead

Again armed exclusively for OCA, a 494th FS F-15E departs Incirlik at the start of yet another ONW patrol. The unit completed two *Provide Comfort II*, two ONW and one OSW deployments between August 1993 and May 2001 (*USAF*)

Left and below
The AGM-130 was a stand-off guided munition designed to be flown to the target by the WSO. Upon release, the rocket motor, strapped to the bottom of the bomb, would ignite and sustain the weapon in flight. Beaming back either an IR or Electro-optical imagery to the F-15E via a data link, the bomb was guided by the WSO, who viewed a display from the bomb's seeker similar to the one seen below, to its intended target. Despite the weapon's potential, it has proven less than reliable in combat (*FJPhotography.com*)

and "Gomez" was my backseater. It was a night vision goggles (NVG) mission patrolling the southern No-Fly Zone. I was full of adrenaline, and more alert than I have ever been in my life. My visual lookout was like you read about. It amazed me how many jets were in the container (southern Iraq) at the same time and the same place. The amount of coordination and deconfliction required was impressive.

'Well, whilst flying around that night the Iraqis launched one of their "science project" missiles into the air. All I saw was what looked like a blue firework exploding five miles away from us. For a split-second I thought it looked pretty! But back to reality – it was *not* pretty, but it wasn't too much of a threat either. This was the case with the AAA I saw during that deployment as well.

'I also won't forget my first drop in Iraq. It was actually my first time dropping live weapons, period. We were a four-ship flying around in the container when the higher ups decided to execute us. This basically meant that we could then drop on the pre-planned targets that we had walked out the door with from Al Jaber.

'Sometimes we'd take off with imagery of 3-4 target areas so the powers-that-be would have more options when they executed us, but this time we only had two target areas planned and we dropped on one. And there were only three DMPIs (Desired Mean Point of Impact). Luckily, we were No 2 in the formation and got to drop. "Barney", my backseater, did an excellent job finding the small KS-19 AAA battery amongst the desert background. It felt great when those two GBU-12s came off the jet. And the explosion when they hit the AAA piece was awesome. So this is what we practise in training all the time! It really all came down to luck as to whether you dropped on that deployment, though.

'The alert sorties we flew down there were pretty cool as well. Sitting all day in a trailer in your flight gear wasn't fun, but when you got scrambled

 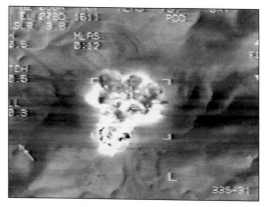

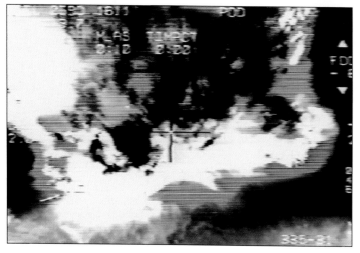

Pod video – also called weapons systems video (WSV) – of the moment that 335th FS WSO Capt Matt Nicoletta's target exploded during his ONW deployment in July 1999. The second frame (top right) shows the initial explosion and the start of the 'blooming' process as the AAQ-14's IR sensor is overwhelmed by the heat of the explosion. By the third screen (above) the fireball is so large that it dominates the entire display. Attacked with a single GBU-10 LGB, this target is suspected to have been a Scud propellant storage plant (*USAF via Matt Nicoletta*)

the excitement more than made up for the hours of boredom. We would get the call on the "Bat Phone" that we were scrambled. Then we would race into the back of the truck and haul ass out to the jets. When we got to the jets, we would jump out, run up the ladder into the cockpit and start up as we were strapping in. In 2-3 minutes we'd be ready to taxi out and take-off.

'There is one particular alert sortie I will never forget as well. It occurred after sitting alert for 12 hours and already being scrambled once. "Mojo" was my backseater and "Killer" and "Flak" were our flight lead. We got the second call and raced off. I had some problems with my EGI (our embedded GPS) on the ground, but nothing that couldn't be resolved after take-off. After take-off my INS (Inertial Navigation System) failed and could not be fixed. The two systems were shorting each other out, so no matter what we did, neither one would work.

'While we were trying to fix our navigation and attitude systems our flight controls started acting up. We ended up losing our CAS (Control Augmentation System) as well. That wasn't too big a deal – it just meant we had slightly degraded control. Then my HUD started showing incorrect information. In level flight it had us 20 degrees nose high and in 5-10 degrees of bank. Nothing could fix this problem so I turned it off.

'After we had burnt down enough gas to land it was well into the night. The primary runway (the one with lights) at Al Jaber was closed, so we had to land on the taxiway (also known as the secondary runway) which had no approach area and very little lighting. We ended up flying a no CAS, HUD out formation approach to land on our squadron CO's wing that night. "Mojo" and I were just happy to be on the ground.'

Capt Matt Nicoletta, who participated in the 335th FS's sole ONW AEF deployment in July 1999, recalled a truly memorable mission;

'On my first ONW sortie I was shot at – seeing three white trails to my left, I said "Missile in the air, 11 o'clock, check right". My pilot, who had

more experience than me, replied, "Dude, those are roads, not missiles!" As I kept watching them, these "roads" began to arc towards us! I said, "Missile in the air, check right, NOW!" My front seater looked at them once more and realised that they were indeed missiles – we broke right and evaded them, although I don't know if they would have hit us anyway. The radios then came alive as everyone started their threat reaction, and I realised that what I should have done was told the whole formation about the missiles!

'Red Flag prepared me for all of the ONW missions responses, but it was still an interesting experience. Sometimes we responded by striking back at the SAM sites, or hitting another target. We did fly with pre-set targets for retaliatory strikes, although command and control would have to authorise us before we did anything. Our typical load-outs included GBU-12s, GBU-10s, AGM-130s, AIM-120s and AIM-9s.

'We executed several pre-planned attacks when we were there. On one occasion we were being shot at with AAA, so we used GBU-10s to hit what we had been told was an ammunition bunker.

'I was used to the size of the GBU-12 explosion, but as the bomb hit this big square bunker I thought "that looks big even for a GBU-10". I went to WFOV and the explosion still filled up my entire screen! The radios then went mad, everyone saying "Holy Cow, what did you just hit!?" I looked out of the window and just thought "Oh my God!". There was this huge, billowing mushroom cloud rocketing up through 7000 ft that had sucked up so much dirt that the sky began to darken as it extended up beyond 15,000 ft. My pilot transmitted, "One hell of a secondary!", which was a huge understatement because the explosion was so big that we had to cancel the rest of the day's bombing!

'No one told us what it was, but it sounds cool to tell everyone that we hit a Scud propellant storage plant! The video shows an overpressure which was so powerful that a large hill next to the target was sucked up into the mushroom cloud. We liked to joke that Intel probably classified our target as "Possibly Damaged!".'

Nicoletta also recalled that the 335th FS struck an SA-6 during the same deployment.

Continuation training was key to the Strike Eagle crews' ability to remain skilled at their jobs whilst on deployment. For those units based in Saudi Arabia (OSW) and Turkey (ONW), there was the inevitability that with the host nation completely controlling their flying schedule, there would be a degradation in skills. For those located elsewhere – in Kuwait, Bahrain or Oman, for example – there were fewer restrictions in place, and the flying was plentiful. Two 391st FS jets regroup over the desert after one such sortie (*Gary Klett via Author*)

DENY FLIGHT AND ALLIED FORCE

Operation *Deny Flight* (ODF) centered on the enforcement of a United Nations' No-Fly Zone over the Republic of Bosnia-Herzegovina. Relations between ethnic groups in the Balkans had deteriorated consistently over many years, but it was not until 1992 that UN peace keeping troops moved in to restore peace, and a No-Fly Zone to protect them was correspondingly authorised under UN Security Council Resolution 781.

On 31 March 1993, the UN Security Council passed Resolution 816, which extended the ban to cover flights by all fixed-wing and rotary-wing aircraft except those authorised by the UN Protection Force (UNPROFOR), and, in the event of further violations, authorised UN member states to take all necessary measures to ensure compliance.

ODF, which was the resolution's primary enforcement operation, began on 12 April 1993 and included eight F-15Es from the 492nd FS 'Bolars' flying from Aviano air base, in Italy. The unit was supported by a small detachment from its sister-squadron, the 494th FS. Under NATO command, both units remained in Italy for more than a year.

ODF was initially undertaken by some 50 UN member state fighter and reconnaissance aircraft, and this force was later increased in size to more than 100 aircraft. By late 1993 the situation in the Balkans had worsened, forcing NATO to order a limited strike against Serbian targets in Croatia, and in particular Udbina airfield. Eight 492nd F-15Es, armed with GBU-12s, sortied as part of a 30-aircraft strike package. Their target was the destruction of SA-6 SAM sites, although the mission was cancelled mid-flight as the gaggle of Strike Eagles were unable to prosecute the attack due to stringent rules of engagement (ROE).

F-15Es from both 48th FW squadrons at RAF Lakenheath deployed to Aviano air base for Operation *Deny Flight* in April 1993. F-15E 90-0248 is seen here armed with inert Mk 82 AIR retarded bombs during a training mission soon after the deployment had commenced. This aircraft was the very first F-15E delivered to the 48th FW in February 1992, the jet arriving at Lakenheath in wing commander's colours. It remained marked up in this scheme until sent back to the USA in February 2000 and transferred to the 90th FS at Elmendorf AFB. 90-0248 was passed on to the 391st FS/366th AW in July 2002, and it is still currently operated by this unit (*Gary Klett via Author*)

Once again, F-15Es were launched in December 1993 to destroy a pair of SA-2 SAM sites which had recently fired upon two Royal Navy Sea Harrier FRS 1s, but for the most part many of the missions were nondescript in nature. Lt Col Michael Arnold deployed to Aviano with the 492nd FS in the summer of 1994, and he recalled;

'At that time I was in Blue Squadron (492nd FS), and most of the missions we flew were very benign and very dull. We enforced the No-Fly Zone, so we would go up and try and engage anyone who was not supposed to be flying, but of course we never saw anything. We did fly some on-call CAS (Close Air Support) with the NATO AWACS that was down there – "Disney" and "Windmill" were the two main AWACS call-signs – but it was basically like doing a whole load of practice. We sometimes carried CBUs, but mostly it was GBU-12s. I never dropped a weapon over there, but I did get shot at a couple of times!

'We were flying along at night and I saw the missile coming up and turning into the "doughnut of fire" – where the SAM comes up, points at you and then the middle of the exhaust plume is blacked out by the missile body as it comes towards you. We did not have NVGs at that time, so when the missile rocket motor burned out we lost sight of it and continued to fly a "no sight" defence. It was unnerving.'

The on-call CAS was run primarily by 'Bookshelf', a C-130 Airborne Command, Control and Communications platform. Arnold explained;

'Bookshelf' would tell you who to talk to, and would also talk to the individual units on the ground to decide who needed air support, and how best to use it. CAS was very new to us back then – we would hold up the little section in our tactics manual and it would say, "we don't do CAS", but they soon changed it. Our ex-F-16, A-10 and Air Liaison Officers made it easier to adapt, and helped devise the tactics we needed.'

A more robust enforcement of ODF commenced in August 1995 following the Serbian mortar-shelling of a market square in Sarajevo. The 90th FS subsequently deployed from Elmendorf for several months, joining the 492nd and 494th FSs who already had eight jets apiece in-theatre and had flown well over 2500 sorties since ODF had begun more than two years earlier. Just under 2000 of these sorties were attributed to the 492nd FS, which had been deployed for longer.

Five punitive strikes hit Serbian armour and supplies around Sarajevo on 30 August, and 24 hours later three targets were bombed. GBU-10s and GBU-12s were again dropped by Lakenheath F-15Es on 5 September as the strikes became more widespread. Four days later, the GBU-15 EO-guided glide bomb was dropped for the very first time in anger by the F-15E – nine were used in total to strike air defence targets and Bosnian-Serb ground forces around Banja Luca.

The Boeing GBU-15 had initially started life in 1974 as a solution to the requirement for a stand-off precision guided bomb. Carried on the F-15E during phase test and evaluation in March 1988, the weapon

The 2000-lb GBU-15 EO-guided glide bomb proved to be particularly effective against Serbian AAA and SAM sites during both ODF and OAF (*USAF*)

The 90th FS fell under the command of the 3rd Wing at Elmendorf AFB, in Alaska. As part of Pacific Air Forces (PACAF), it was exempt from AEF rotations and therefore deployed to combat zones less often than ACC and USAFE Strike Eagle squadrons. Even so, it did participate in ODF in August 1995, deploying to support the two Lakenheath squadrons. Needless to say, the unit did not get to employ its AIM-7Ms whilst in the Balkans (*USAF*)

combined an EO DSU-27A/B seeker head with one of two IR seeker heads – the WGU-33/B, which offered correlation tracking, or the WGU-10/B, which was limited to centroid tracking only. All three could be mated to a BLU-109 or Mk 84 2000-lb bomb body.

Several basic variations were used. The GBU-15S had a short chord wing and was designated GBU-15(V)31/B when attached to an IR seeker or GBU-15(V)32/B with the EO head, while the GBU-15L featured a long chord wing and comprised the GBU-15(V)1/B, 1A/B and 1B/B when fitted with the EO seeker head. Finally, the GBU-15(V)2/B, 2A/B and 2B/B featured either IR seeker.

Direct mode allowed the bomb to be locked onto the target prior to launch, and once released, it would guide autonomously. Indirect mode made use of either an AXQ-14 datalink pod (DLP) or ZSW-1 Improved DL Pod (IDLP) with which to steer the weapon post-launch. A training round, known as the SUU-59, was carried (minus wings) for training.

Launching the GBU-15 proved a simple matter, as steering cues and range indications were provided in the HUD and on the GBU-15 Video MPD page. The bomb could be cued from the radar, HUD or TP, and released in either climbing or level profiles. In Indirect mode its seeker could be slewed via the DL to acquire the target as the bomb flew within visual range – the WSO slewed the seeker onto the target, and then committed the bomb to attacking it – a process which caused the bomb's control fins to bring its line-of-fall in line with the seeker line-of-sight.

To help the WSO, the GBU-15 offered a Ground Stabilisation option. As the bomb flew out to the target area in Indirect mode, the WSO was initially limited to steering the weapon in azimuth only – this prevented him from inadvertently depleting the weapon's kinetic energy through unnecessary pitch changes. During this time the weapon completed a 'terminal manoeuvre' intended to bring it within striking range of the target. The WSO could take control of pitch steering at any time by switching the bomb from 'transition mode' to 'terminal mode'.

The GBU-15 featured GPS midcourse guidance, allowing the crew to release the weapon in poor visibility. The bomb would drive itself to the pre-entered target coordinates, taking steering commands from an onboard GPS receiver. Once in the target area, the WSO could take control via the DLP as normal. Lakenheath crews returned to the UK with spectacular video of their GBU-15 exploits – in one instance a man

45

could be seen running from an SA-6 moments before the weapon impacted directly onto the target.

The 494th FS deployed once more to Aviano air base for Operation *Deliberate Guard* (ODG), six aircraft departing RAF Lakenheath on 30 September 1997 and returning on 13 January 1998 when an identical number of 492nd FS jets arrived to replace them – the latter stayed in Italy for just over a month. Immediately upon the 494th's return home, the unit began preparations for an AEF deployment to Turkey for ONW.

DELIBERATE GUARD AND ALLIED FORCE

ODG was another UN-mandated No-Fly Zone effort in the airspace over Bosnia-Herzegovina. Months later, in early 1999, Operation *Allied Force* (OAF) was launched following the displacement of some 300,000 refugees from Kosovo. After repeated warnings by NATO to Serbian President Slobodan Milosevic to remove his forces from Kosovo were ignored, the first Balkan AEF force arrived, including six 492nd FS jets.

A five-phase plan was put into effect, whereby NATO flights would initially act as a deterrent, before becoming more aggressive if NATO demands were not met. Despite gains made at the Rambouillet peace talks in France, 12 more F-15Es from the 492nd FS were sent to Italy on 22 January 1999 as part of an operation code named *Noble Anvil*.

The bombing phase of *Noble Anvil* commenced on the night of 24 March 1999 when, in the wake of several Conventional Air-Launched Cruise Missile strikes by B-52s, all 26 F-15Es in-theatre concentrated on striking SAM, AAA and GCI Early Warning (EW) assets as they followed behind a wall of Lakenheath F-15Cs flying OCA sorties.

As the conflict progressed, Strike Eagle crews turned their hand to dropping CBUs and other types of weapons, including the GBU-28A/B bunker-penetrating LGB. Originally developed for F-111F crews during *Desert Storm*, the GBU-28 could penetrate through 100 ft of concrete before exploding. It consisted of a BLU-113 bomb body with a WGU-36/B laser guidance kit and BSG-92/B airfoil group. The GBU-28A/B featured

Armed with AIM-120C AMRAAMs and AIM-9Ms, a pair of 492nd FS jets soak up the sun at Aviano air base during the unit's 1995 ODF deployment. Amongst the first jets assigned to the 48th FW in May 1992, 90-0256 served with the wing until transferred to the 57th Wing in October 1999 – it is still being used by the training unit today. 91-0301 remains with the 492nd FS, having been flown by the squadron since August 1992 (*USAF*)

The pilot of bombed up 494th FS F-15E 92-0364 waits for clearance to taxi onto the runway at the start of an early OAF mission from Aviano in March 1999. This aircraft is also another 494th FS veteran with over a decade of USAFE service to its credit (*USAF*)

A 492nd FS F-15E releases a GBU-28 'bunker busting' LGB during bomb trials in the USA. This weapon, which can penetrate 100 ft of concrete before exploding, was used in March 1999 during OEF. Interestingly, this 'Mad Hatters' jet shows four bomb markings below the canopy. These symbols almost certainly denote recent action seen by the jet in the Balkans theatre (*USAF*)

both an expanded launch envelope and an advanced Guidance and Control Unit which took into account target pressure altitude to ensure that the weapon struck the aim point at a minimum angle of attack – this enhanced penetration characteristics. The weapon was used, unsuccessfully, in *Noble Anvil* against an underground hangar at Pristina air base. Lt Col Will Reece was the 492nd FS's Weapons Officer at the time;

'I initially stayed at Lakenheath supporting operations in the Mission Planning Cell (MPC). We communicated primarily through Aviano's MPC – informally called "The Wingtip", as Lakenheath's MPC was known as "The Claw" – because they had the majority of the assets.

'NATO and the American forces had planned on President Milosevic capitulating after three days, but when you look back at that country's culture and history, and with 20-20 vision, how wrong were we to have thought that?! You can understand why the Serbs laughed at that assumption. We had a big concern about collateral damage, and that shows when you look at the targets we hit, and how we hit them.

'Air operations in *Allied Force* had two main aims. The first was interdiction in order to keep the Serbian Army out of Kosovo – any roads, bridges or routes to let them into Kosovo were taken out, and our target sets extended some way outside of Kosovo to make that happen. The second was CAS, and we (492nd and 494th FSs) were the only two Strike Eagle units in the Air Force practising that mission. Although CAS is now flown throughout the USAF, it was very new to us in 1999.'

With the conflict escalating, in May 1999 the 48th FW mounted offensive operations from Lakenheath for the first time since the 1986 F-111F raid on Libya. These missions supplemented sorties being flown by the F-15Es from Aviano air base.

Lt Col Michael Arnold, who had participated in ODF five years earlier, was serving an In-Place Continuous Overseas Tour at this time, allowing him to stay at Lakenheath well beyond the usual three-year stint. He was one of the aircrew to fly sorties from the Strike Eagles' home base;

'Most of these flights lasted about 7.5 hours and included two aerial refuellings. The most difficult part of these missions was working with the civilian air traffic agencies on the way over! We flew there, refuelled, hit the target and then went home. The aircraft were usually armed with a GBU-10 and GBU-24, or a couple of GBU-12s and a GBU-24. We'd also be carrying two tanks and an air-to-air missile load.'

Flying these lengthy missions over hostile territory before returning home to Lakenheath was an odd experience, as Arnold explained;

'It was strange. Weird. Everything was at night, but it was all very comfortable. We'd take off well after "quiet hours", but when we landed we'd have a drink in our own squadron pub, then go home and climb into our own beds. It was surreal, and it didn't seem like we were at war.'

And what of the impact on his wife, living in the Suffolk countryside?

'I don't think she noticed or realised exactly what I was doing! She didn't connect the two. Every day, I was going out there with the potential to be shot down, but I didn't think about it that way either'.

The F-15E was the only allied aircraft to operate in all weathers, day or night, and *Allied Force* saw the Strike Eagle community use NVGs in combat for the very first time. One other significant change was the dual role of the F-15E during the conflict, as the the AIM-120C enabled the F-15E to come off target and revert immediately to a CAP role. Using this tactic, crews could protect the rest of the strikers as they attacked their target.

On several occasions crews did not have NVGs, so they worked with NVG-equipped F-16s to buddy-lase. Buddy-lasing involved F-15Es dropping GBUs which would be guided onto the target by the F-16's own TP. Lt Col Arnold also recalled instances where CAP was flown for a few hours, following which the flight would strike a pre-planned target before returning home. The Balkans conflict provided the Strike Eagle community with ample opportunity to flex its multi-role muscles.

THE MOBILE THREAT

Much of the Federal Republic of Yugoslavia Air Force and Air Defence Force derived their tactics from standard Soviet operating procedures, and in this sense they were no different from Iraq. Where they did differ was in their conviction to use their military might against a superior force like NATO, and the fact that they had links to Iraq which they had exploited to learn US military secrets and tactics.

It came as no surprise to F-15E crews arriving at Aviano that their threat briefing apportioned considerable time to defining the capabilities of a largely mobile SAM environment. The main problem was a large contingent of highly mobile SA-6 launchers, which rarely stayed in one location for long as they supplemented vulnerable fixed SA-2/3 sites. Indeed, Milosevic's forces were cunning in their use of deception and in their self-control – they hid several of these potent systems, resisting the urge to fire until conditions were in their favour. Lt Col Reece explained;

'There are a lot of processes in our planning that we go through in order to identify what our targets are, and where we can expect to find them. We have some smart folks who tell us where they think the threats are, but the Serbs were very smart too, and they had learned a lot from the Iraqis. They moved their systems around, and so sometimes it was very difficult to know exactly where the SA-6s were. We sometimes got surprised, but the reality is that with the systems we have in the F-15E, I can beat an SA-6 if I can see it. It's the one that I can't see that's going to get me.

'I started off flying F-111s, where the employment philosophy was totally different. In this jet we were going to go low, hide from the threats and kill our target before scrambling our way out. In the F-15E, the mentality is totally different – I'm here, bring it on, as I'm not necessarily going to hide. Of course, we don't put ourselves unnecessarily at risk, but now when we're targeted by these older systems we're more confident.'

On 2 June 1995 F-16C pilot Capt Scott O'Grady had been downed by an SA-6 near Bosanki, in Bosnia, whilst on a routine patrol. Whilst this shoot-down was attributed largely to pilot error, it is highly likely that he also flew into a SAM trap – a tactic which used (*text continues on page 58*)

COLOUR PLATES

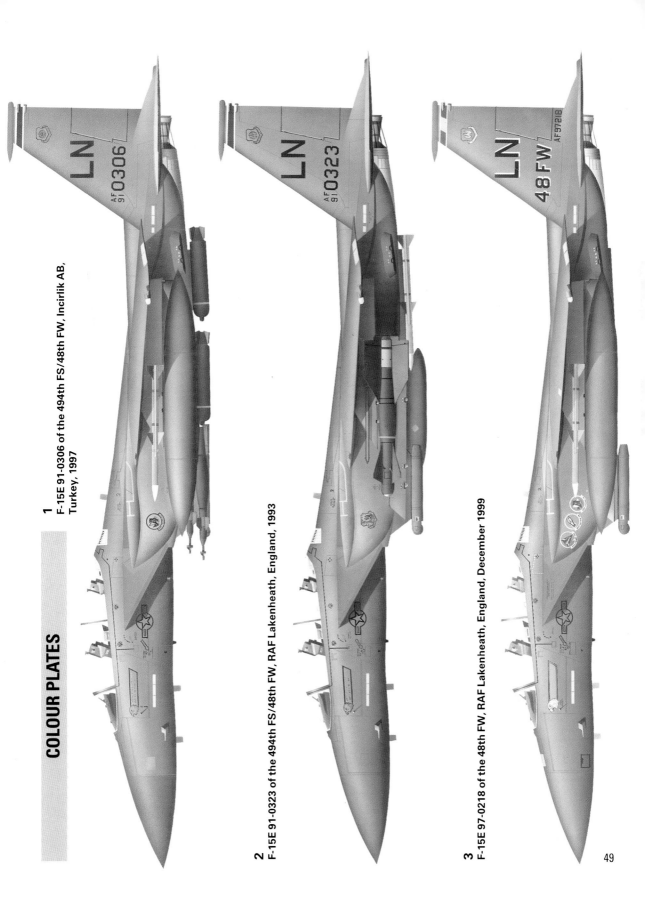

1
F-15E 91-0306 of the 494th FS/48th FW, Incirlik AB,
Turkey, 1997

2
F-15E 91-0323 of the 494th FS/48th FW, RAF Lakenheath, England, 1993

3
F-15E 97-0218 of the 48th FW, RAF Lakenheath, England, December 1999

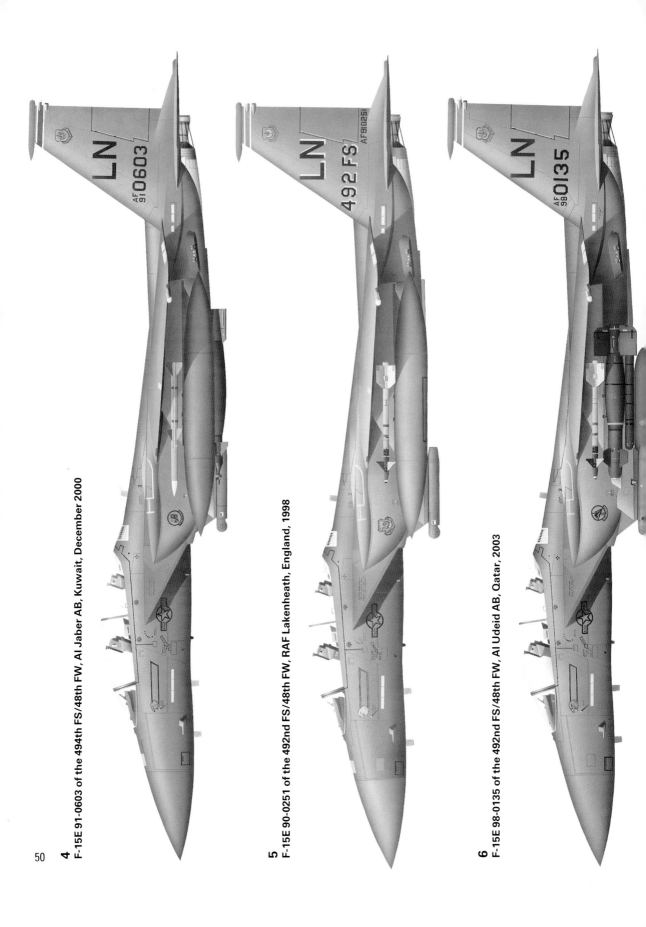

4
F-15E 91-0603 of the 494th FS/48th FW, Al Jaber AB, Kuwait, December 2000

5
F-15E 90-0251 of the 492nd FS/48th FW, RAF Lakenheath, England, 1998

6
F-15E 98-0135 of the 492nd FS/48th FW, Al Udeid AB, Qatar, 2003

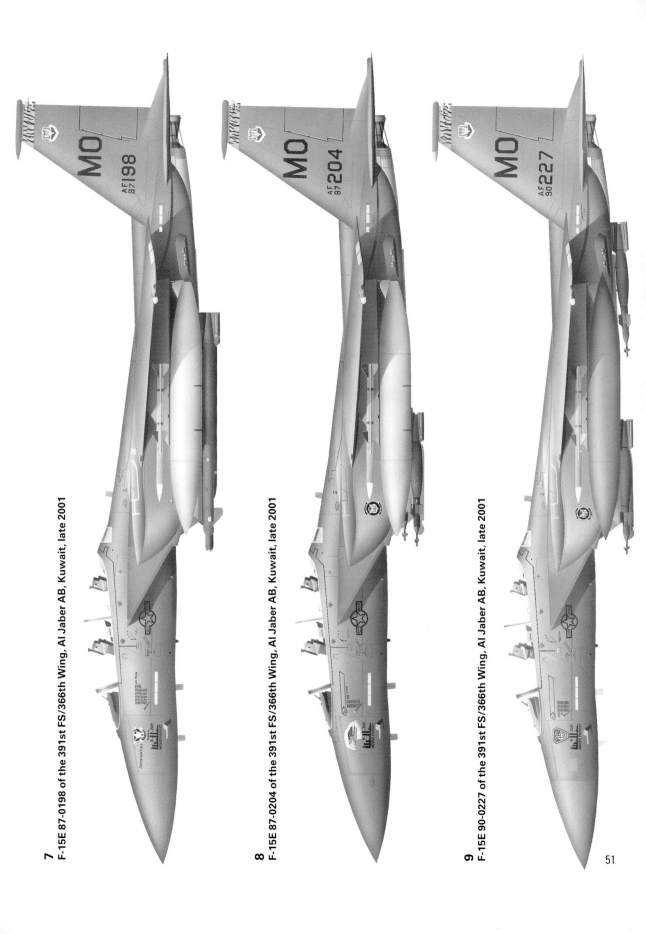

7
F-15E 87-0198 of the 391st FS/366th Wing, Al Jaber AB, Kuwait, late 2001

8
F-15E 87-0204 of the 391st FS/366th Wing, Al Jaber AB, Kuwait, late 2001

9
F-15E 90-0227 of the 391st FS/366th Wing, Al Jaber AB, Kuwait, late 2001

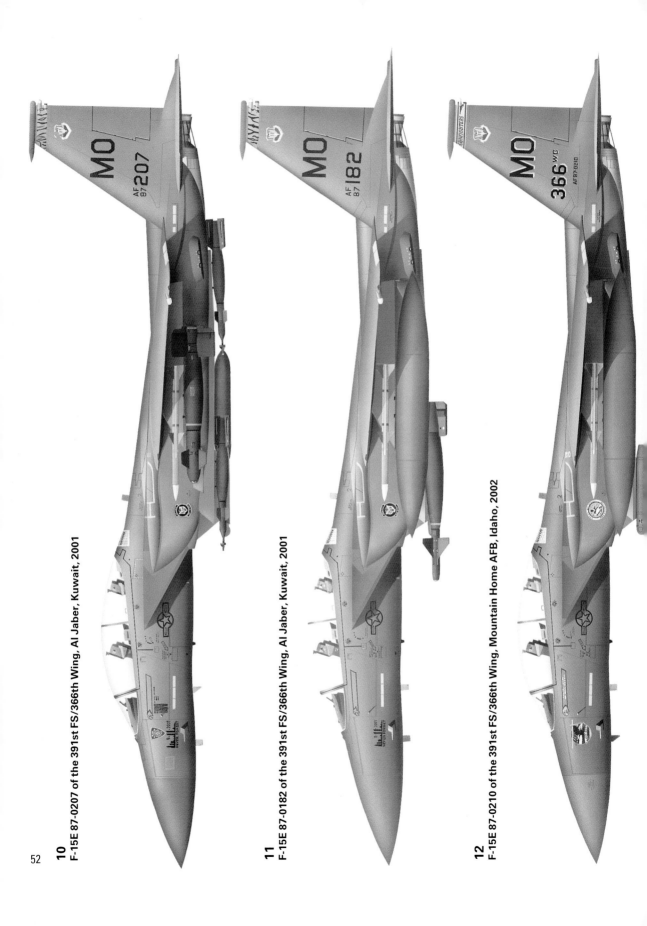

10
F-15E 87-0207 of the 391st FS/366th Wing, Al Jaber, Kuwait, 2001

11
F-15E 87-0182 of the 391st FS/366th Wing, Al Jaber, Kuwait, 2001

12
F-15E 87-0210 of the 391st FS/366th Wing, Mountain Home AFB, Idaho, 2002

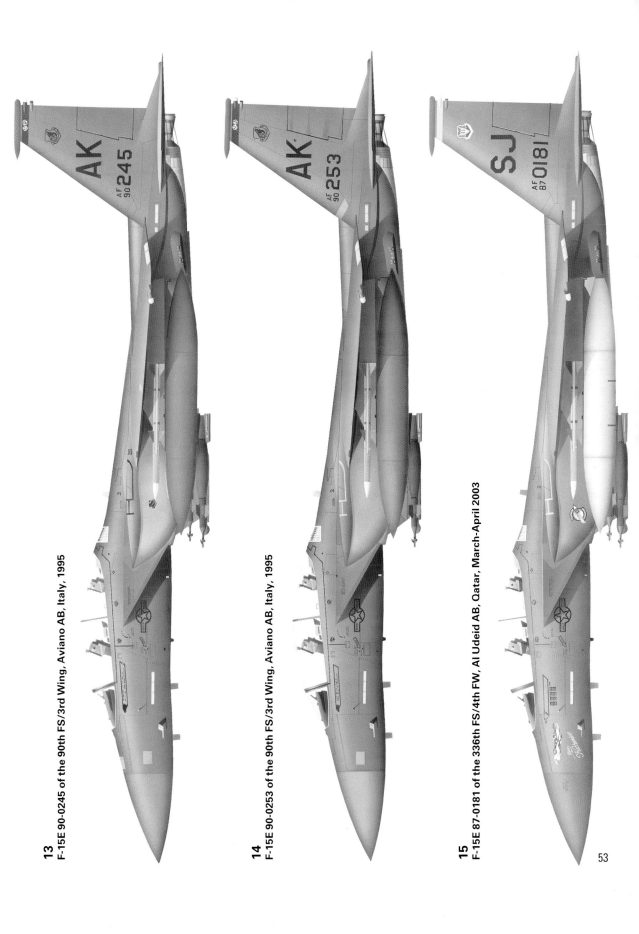

13
F-15E 90-0245 of the 90th FS/3rd Wing, Aviano AB, Italy, 1995

14
F-15E 90-0253 of the 90th FS/3rd Wing, Aviano AB, Italy, 1995

15
F-15E 87-0181 of the 336th FS/4th FW, Al Udeid AB, Qatar, March–April 2003

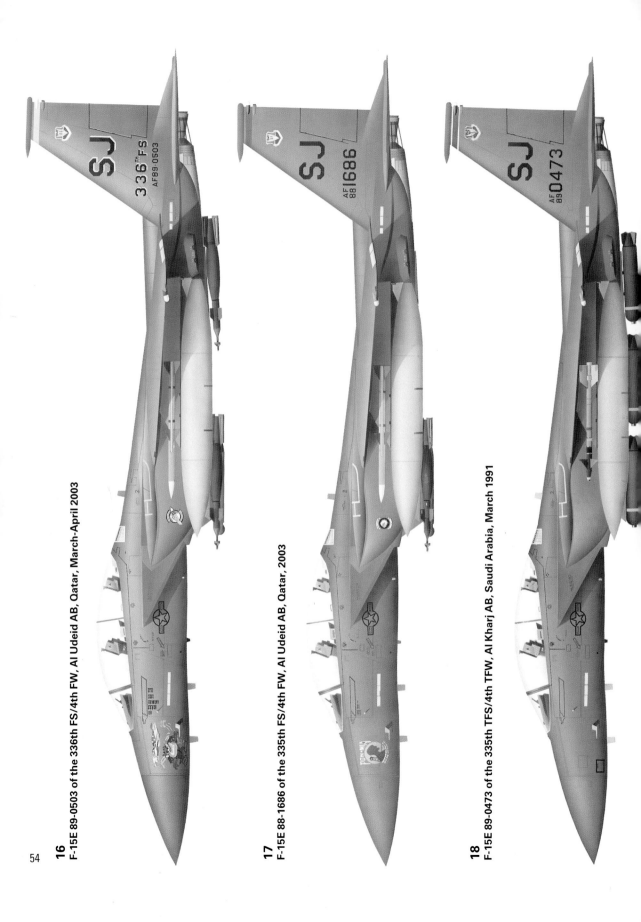

16
F-15E 89-0503 of the 336th FS/4th FW, Al Udeid AB, Qatar, March-April 2003

17
F-15E 88-1686 of the 335th FS/4th FW, Al Udeid AB, Qatar, 2003

18
F-15E 89-0473 of the 335th TFS/4th TFW, Al Kharj AB, Saudi Arabia, March 1991

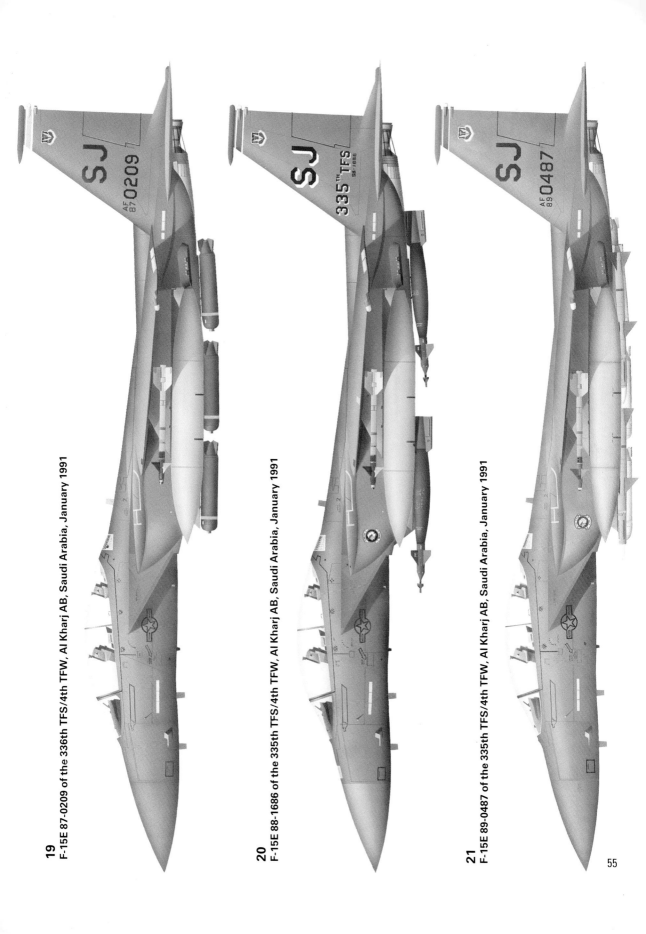

19
F-15E 87-0209 of the 336th TFS/4th TFW, Al Kharj AB, Saudi Arabia, January 1991

20
F-15E 88-1686 of the 335th TFS/4th TFW, Al Kharj AB, Saudi Arabia, January 1991

21
F-15E 89-0487 of the 335th TFS/4th TFW, Al Kharj AB, Saudi Arabia, January 1991

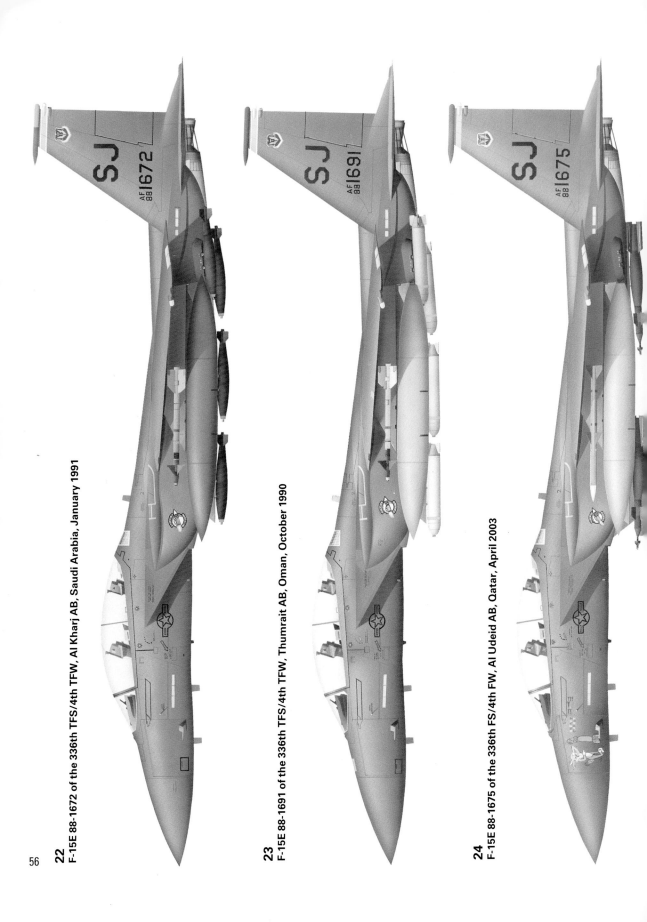

22
F-15E 88-1672 of the 336th TFS/4th TFW, Al Kharj AB, Saudi Arabia, January 1991

23
F-15E 88-1691 of the 336th TFS/4th TFW, Thumrait AB, Oman, October 1990

24
F-15E 88-1675 of the 336th FS/4th FW, Al Udeid AB, Qatar, April 2003

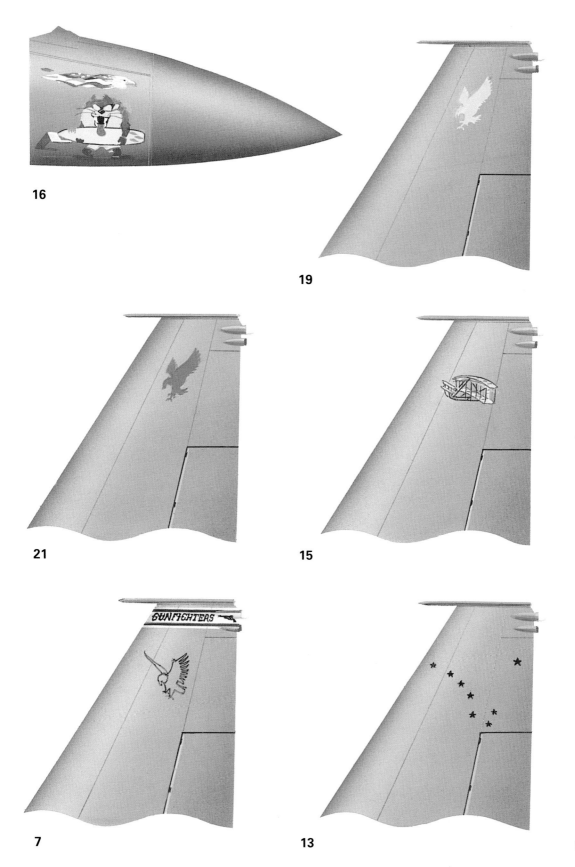

16

19

21

15

7

13

two or more mobile SAM systems to target the same aircraft from different locations, and was made possible because NATO jets were assigned the same routes day after day. During seven years of operations in the Balkans, a French Mirage 2000 had also been downed, so too had an Italian G222 and a Royal Navy Sea Harrier FRS 1. Most notable of all, however, was the loss of an F-117 stealth fighter, which was also downed because NATO planners failed to alter its egress and ingress tracks.

By contrast, the F-15E community emerged from the OAF campaign without suffering a single loss, although there were certainly occasions when things could have turned out for the worse, as 'Skull' explained;

'Their surface-to-air systems were robust and widespread, making it difficult to know where they all were – the mobile SAMs were the biggest concern. We initially flew CAP sorties until March, but we were never given a date for when we would switch to offensive ops. My first sortie was a CAP/CAS on Day Three of the war, carrying four GBU-12s, two AIM-7 and two AIM-120. We were on station defending Italy against any attacks, although we knew that the Serbs posed little threat as their jets didn't have the range to get home should they attempt such a mission.

'We (492nd FS) flew night after night – I flew almost every other night. When the weather stopped us from using PGMs, we would drop Mk 82s with proximity fuses and CBU-87s on area targets like ammunition storage facilities and troop concentrations – we were always well away from civilian areas when we did this.

'One night we were egressing a target when we received audio and visual indications of an SA-6 launch. They launched two to begin with – we think that they had an ambush site underneath us. I rolled the jet upside down and pulled towards one of the missiles. It passed by so closely that my WSO thought I had popped a flare. We then had this impromptu little "discussion" about whether I had or not! We resolved it by looking at the TEWS page which showed that we still had a full quantity of flares onboard.

'A third SAM was launched when the first two petered out, and once again I rolled into it and it flew by too close for comfort. As we climbed up to altitude, they shot two more at us from an adjacent site ten miles to the east, but we still had good airspeed and I defeated them too. For these latter SAMs we got no TEWS indications, and we concluded that they had attempted a visual launch.

The mobility of the SA-6 (below) and its 'Straight Flush' radar (bottom) allowed President Milosevic's forces to operate the SAM fleetingly and when the conditions were in their favour. The weapon featured an optical guidance mode that was apparently used frequently during OAF (*FAS.org*)

'Surprisingly, we were both calm. I was lucky because my WSO, Maj Willis, was a *Desert Storm* veteran who had been shot at before. It was a surreal experience, as they looked like fireworks – they were beautiful. In some senses it was almost mesmerising. I remember asking Maj Willis, "Hey, is that a missile left, ten o'clock?" He looked and responded with an emphatic "Yes!"'

Lt Col Arnold had similar memories;

'I remember that both times I was shot at, I am ashamed to say that the first words out of my mouth were "Oh shit!", instead of saying something directive like "Check 30° right!" or "Chaff! Chaff!" The second time it was AAA, and it came up just off our right wing. My initial thoughts were "Hey, that's neat", before I actually said "Holy Shit! They're shooting at us, right, three o'clock".'

Arnold was also apprehensive prior to flying his first OAF missions;

'I was thinking that this was the real deal. These guys have a real IADS, are really trained and this could be very difficult.'

As it turned out, he reflected, Serbian IADS posed less of a threat than he had originally thought they would. Additionally, there was no hint of a kamikaze mindset to flying into harm's way amongst F-15E crews. Lt Col Reece rationalised it thus;

'We defined what was too risky in terms of actual risk levels. We would take a look at the objectives and then compare them with the risk levels that the Air Component Commander was prepared to accept. If I could work my way around a threat then we may still have been able to meet those risk levels, but in some scenarios the target was not worth the risk, and we would determine that it was not worth the loss of a jet or a person. It was a complex, constantly evolving process that you didn't normally hear about at aircrew level, but it was considered and looked at every day by the squadron commander.'

STAYING OUT OF THE MEZ

When the threat was too high to penetrate, or specific weapons effects were required, the AGM-130 was used to provide increased stand-off distance from the target. Having debuted without success in Iraq during ONW that same year, the AGM-130 successfully destroyed two MiG-29s on the ground in OAF. Lt Col Reece explained;

'Because they're so expensive, you use the AGM-130 and GBU-15 against very specific targets. During OAF, the threats were so unpredictable that we evolved from what was historically a large planning effort to a flexible mentality. So, there was not nearly as much planning as there had been in the past. The AGM-130 used a modified GBU-15 as the basis for an extended range PGM. A rocket motor was mounted to the underside of the GBU-15 to provide the bomb with a glide-boost-glide operating profile. The motor was intended to maintain a desired minimum velocity, rather than to accelerate the bomb. Once the motor expired, it was jettisoned automatically.

'AGM-130-9/-10/-11/-12 variants also featured a GPS mid-course guidance system, which allowed the bomb to navigate itself towards the target area. The latter two versions also had an antenna installed in the bomb to help increase data link reception coverage – this feature is known as Switchable Data Link. EO and IR versions of the AGM-130 use the

WGU-40/B TV Guidance Section and WGU-42/B Improved Modular Infra Red Sensor (IMIRS) seeker heads respectively. IMIRS bombs mated to the BLU-109 warhead were designated AGM-130C-10 or AGM-130C-12SDL, while TVGS and BLU-109 bombs were designated AGM-130C-9 or AGM-130C-11SDL.

The weapon functioned in a similar manner to the GBU-15, although the AGM-130 could be programmed with its own transit altitude which would allow target ingress down to 200 ft or up to 2000 ft. The central computer automatically calculated the Dynamic Launch Zone based on the user selection, a missile-mounted radar altimeter provided elevation data and the IR sensor made use of a nitrogen-cooled Focal Plane Array which featured two additional tracking modes (Black and White).

When the weapon was deployed in Indirect mode, the aircrew could designate a target in the jet via the FLIR or radar. This target data would be transmitted to the AGM-130, which would compute the target location relative to its own. A small triangle would subsequently be superimposed over the AGM-130 video in the cockpit to provide the WSO with steering cues to help him guide the weapon to the target. N/WFOVs were provided for enhanced target acquisition purposes.

As Lt Col Reece pointed out, 'the key to the AGM-130 is that it provides a man-in-the-loop facility from the moment the bomb is released to the moment it impacts. With the weapon beaming imagery back to the jet, you're constantly getting closer to the target, so you can really hit it where you want. It allows us to get the effects we need, and nothing more, so we mitigate the impact of the weapon on civilians or nearby buildings etc.'

Whether by day or night, clement or inclement weather, the F-15E proved to be the most tenacious and dependable of airframes during the operations in the Balkans theatre. When other assets were grounded due to weather, it was the Strike Eagle that ventured into the unknown and continued to execute the mission, despite the increased dangers associated with flying over enemy territory in such conditions (*Gary Klett via Author*)

AGM-130 launches were usually undertaken with two jets monitoring video imagery beamed back via the AXQ-14 or ZSW-1 DLP/IDLP. In the event that the primary jet was unable to locate the target in a timely manner, the secondary F-15E was used as fall back. The primary would typically transmit 'Goalkeeper, Goalkeeper' as a cue for the secondary crew to take control of the missile.

Video imagery from the AGM-130 during OAF shows the launch jet up to 50 miles from the target at the time of weapon impact. This range does not accurately reflect the true stand-off range offered by the missile, however, as the launch aircraft would invariably turn 180 degrees following the launch (in order to remain distant from the threats invariably surrounding the target). Despite this, it gave a clear indication as to the capabilities of the weapon and DLP, which featured a rear facing, mechanically steered Phase Scanned Array antenna to allow continued communication with the bomb as it flew in the opposite direction.

It was an AGM-130 that struck a bridge just as a passenger train crossed it, resulting in a large loss of civilian lives. This event prompted massive condemnation from the world's media, but as Lt Col Reece explained when interviewed in January 2005, every effort had been made by NATO and the F-15E crew who guided the bomb to avoid such an incident;

'On an operational level there is a great deal of effort that goes into reducing collateral damage. We do everything we can to mitigate the impact on innocent civilians. We will purposely alter the times we strike particular targets to avoid civilian casualties, even if that means us being in greater danger. We follow the International Laws of Armed Conflict and the Geneva Convention to avoid collateral damage. I know the crew who flew this mission, and I can tell you that the WSO feels bad to this day about what happened. In their case, all of the information available to them at the time pointed to the fact that striking the bridge when they did was a safe thing to do.'

After this incident, the level of authorisation required for target approval at NATO increased to the point where all 19 member nations had to agree what was to be bombed before it made the ATO. Fewer target sets were released accordingly. But there were equally poignant missions that failed to make the news either because NATO released no details or they were deemed non-newsworthy. Reece explained;

'The Serbs were smart and adaptive and knew that collateral damage was an Achilles heel for us. So, we'd go after targets and, as we came close, started to see things we weren't expecting. A friend of mine was guiding in his AGM-130 towards the target's anticipated location only to find that the target has been moved and it was now sitting in front of a church. He hastily guided the AGM up and over the top of the target, the weapon eventually falling in some fields behind the church. It was very frustrating for him in the end game, but it was against the ROE to hit targets near buildings such as this so he did the right thing and flew the weapon high.'

In June 1999 President Milosevic relented and allowed thousands of displaced Kosovan Albanian refugees to return home. Operation *Joint Guardian* (OJG) was subsequently activated to provide administrative oversight and security to this process, the 492nd FS heading to Aviano on 10 January 2000 for three months with six jets as part of OJG, followed by the 494th FS from 22 May to 23 June that same year.

AFGHAN REBELS

Following the 11 September 2001 terrorist attacks in New York City and Washington, DC, 12 391st FS F-15Es left Idaho 31 days later bound for Ahmed Al Jaber air base, in Kuwait. Stopping in Spain en route, the jets began operations as part of the 332nd Air Expeditionary Group shortly after their arrival in the Middle East. The 'Bold Tigers' had been scheduled to conduct a routine OSW deployment until just 24 hours prior to departure for Al Jaber. Now they were being assigned to Operation *Enduring Freedom* (OEF).

In some respects the 36 391st aircrew (18 pilots and 18 WSOs) were better prepared for this war than might have been imagined. America's tenuous relationship with Afghanistan had not improved since limited cruise missile strikes targeted at Osama Bin Laden were ordered by then-President Bill Clinton in October 1998. In a move most reminiscent of the 4th TFW's exercises of mid 1990, astute planners and 'patch wearers' within the squadron had taken it upon themselves to build up a picture of what kind of targets Afghanistan would provide for F-15E crews.

Working away in the unit's secure vault, planners had pieced together a basic picture which suggested a non-existent air threat and an unsophisticated air defence system consisting of MANPADS (man portable air defence systems) and AAA. Arriving in Kuwait to a somewhat uncertain tasking, they at least had some idea of what they would be up against.

It had been obvious during the 391st's studies that Afghanistan's dilapidated infrastructure would offer few fixed targets of any real value. Indeed, the squadron had specifically trained for the eventuality that much of its work would see it making full use of Forward Air Controllers (FACs), as Lt Col Andrew Britschgi, 391st FS CO, reflected;

'We knew that we'd end up working mostly with FACs if we were ever tasked to strike targets in Afghanistan – we therefore practised that mission regularly over the course of our peacetime schedule. We also knew that our role within any deployment would see us acting as the primary strike asset, and there is no doubt that our training translated well into the way in which we operated over Afghanistan.'

Twelve F-15Es from the 391st FS/366th AEW departed Mountain Home AFB, Idaho, on 12 October 2001 for OEF. 88-1667 was one of those jets to deploy, this recently overhauled ex-4th FW machine having only just been assigned to the 391st FS a week prior to being sent to Al Jaber. In October 2002 the F-15E was transferred to the 90th FS, with whom it presently serves (*Gary Klett via Author*)

Special Forces FACs and USAF/Army ETACs worked closely with F-15E crews in OEF to achieve mission effectiveness (*USAF*)

The 391st FS crews believed that FACs would guide them to mobile targets or TSTs over jam-resistant radios. Time would soon tell how accurate their predictions had been.

The CAOC at McDill AFB, in Florida, built the ATO. In late October 2001 'TJ' led the first wave of 391st FS F-15E attacks, meeting little resistance over the target. As they returned mid-afternoon, the second Strike Eagle wave departed Al Jaber, and so began an almost continuous cycle of F-15E strikes which would run for three months.

'For the first fortnight or so, military buildings, Taliban supply depots, caves and al-Qaeda training camps were the key focus of our attack', commented 'Fang', a highly experienced WSO who had already seen combat in the Balkans and ONW/OSW.

'Crews would receive the "frag" the night before a mission was flown. The guys not scheduled to fly would break out the ATO and plan the next day's sorties throughout the remainder of the night while the assigned crews got their heads' down. When our own resources were inadequate, we used commercial sources such as five-metre resolution satellite imagery obtained from Georgia State University to fill the blanks. CAOC would provide suggestions for weapon types and delivery modes, but on the whole the squadron would run things as we saw best, and only rarely did the CAOC ever "tell" us how to get the job done. Once the sorties had been planned, the guys flying could come in the next morning one hour before their briefing, familiarise themselves with the route, brief the mission and then step to the jets for engine start.'

Both the AGM-130 and EGBU-15 2000-lb bombs were expended in the first weeks of the war against caves leading to underground facilities. They were also used to strike targets which were difficult to identify under normal conditions, or when desired weapons effects were required.

This was the first time that the EGBU-15 had been dropped in anger, and its employment was just one of a number of 'firsts' achieved by the 'Bold Tigers' in Afghanistan. The GBU-24A/B, fitted with the BLU-109 penetrator warhead, was also used for the destruction of reinforced targets and underground Taliban facilities. The GBU-24A guidance unit, fitted to a Mk 84 body, was also dropped. Both variations featured either a WGU-12B/B or WGU-39/B laser guidance kit, which were designed

Groundcrews line the taxiway at Al Jaber as the 391st FS commences its first sortie of OEF just days after arriving in Kuwait on 13 October 2001. This aircraft is armed with nine GBU-12s, two AIM-9Ms and two AIM-120Cs, plus two 610 US gal drop tanks. This load-out quickly became the standard bomb/missile mix for OEF (*USAF*)

A second 391st FS F-15E emerges from its sun shelter at the start of the squadron's first strike mission from Al Jaber in support of US Central Command's execution of OEF. In the first 33 days of the campaign, USAF aircraft flew more than 2800 sorties – about 45 per cent of all OEF sorties (*USAF*)

A WSO from the 391st FS performs his pre-flight check on the GBU-12s attached to the starboard CFT pylons. An identical load of four 500-lb LGBs would be carried on the port CFT too (*USAF*)

to make use of the GBU-24's enhanced low-altitude delivery envelope. The GBU-28 was also used to strike Taliban command and control centres and cave entrances – a total of five were dropped.

Often, the F-15Es operated as two-ship flights alongside two-ship flights of F-16s. 'Spear' recalled;

'The F-16s had VHF radios, (which the Strike Eagle does not), and this made it much easier to talk to civilian ATC agencies, since most didn't closely monitor their UHF. All players like AWACS and the ground FACs had UHF capability, so VHF made things a little easier when going to and from the target area. For the most part, we'd fly as two ships and would link up with the F-16s over Afghanistan. They would often fly separate orbits from us, but we'd share the same tanker. Only rarely did we ever fly as four F-15Es.'

Within weeks the CAOC planners were discovering that they had almost exhausted their list of meaningful fixed targets. From very early on in OEF they had recognised that a growing number of targets were falling into the TST category – targets such as people and vehicles, which could move or hide if they were not attacked within a certain window of opportunity. It was time to change the way in which air assets were tasked.

The Taliban had access to Soviet-made SA-7 and US-made Stinger 'basic' MANPADS, its air force was believed to be non-existent and it had AAA guns of a variety of calibres, but very little of this was radar directed. 'A lot of their AAA was sound activated' said 'Spear', an F-15E pilot with the 391st FS. 'They'd hear us and fire at where we had been, but they never really came close to us'. His CO, Lt Col Britschgi, concurred. 'In the time I was there I did not get locked up by a single hostile radar'.

Fixed SAM sites around such cities as Mazar-I-Sharif and Bagram were struck very early on with precision weapons, although they may not have actually been serviceable to begin with. In all, the Area of Operations was classed as 'low-threat', and this classification is reinforced by the fact that there was not a single instance of an F-15E jettisoning its external fuel tanks – a standard tactic when evasive manoeuvres need to be flown.

Taliban troops who fired their shoulder-launched missiles rarely posed a threat, as most aircraft were well above the 7000-ft engagement zone of these early generation infrared guided missiles. 'Spear' commented that 'the Taliban conserved their missiles early on in the campaign, but, as the war progressed, their frustration mounted and they began to fire more and more'. Lt Col Britschgi reflected that the Taliban and al-Qaeda soldiers were virtually powerless to do defend themselves, and any futile attempt to do so only brought them more misery as their location was quickly pinpointed and bombed by American aircraft.

The Islamic Republic of Iran Air Force launched several sorties to observe proceedings but did not cross the border, and there are no reports from US aircrew of any encounters with Iranian military jets. 'We were told not to take any unnecessary risks' said 'Fang', 'And we had a range of divert fields that we could fly into if we had an IFE (In Flight Emergency) added 'Spear'.

Both of these factors gave comfort to the 'Bold Tigers', for whom an ejection over Afghanistan was a distinctly ugly prospect, as 'Fang' explained. 'We knew that there were huge distances involved in getting to friendly lines, and the fact that Afghanistan is so heavily mined gave us real food for thought'. Whilst specific procedures are classified, it is likely that aircrew were briefed to seek cover and stay put until help arrived. An abundance of US aerial assets in the region, complete air dominance, lack of any credible form of SAM threat and an inexhaustible supply of tankers would have greatly increased the chances that any downed fliers would be quickly rescued.

As had been predicted, and some three weeks into the operation, the 391st FS's tasking changed from specific targets to providing on-call support for pre-set 'vulnerability' times. 'Fang' compared the system in Afghanistan with those that he had previously experienced;

'The US Army had established a grid system worked out according to Army placement of FACs. It was far better than the East/West system used in Kosovo – we had very specific areas of responsibility here. Our new tasking was geared explicitly to making sure that Time Sensitive Tasking targets could be hit as expeditiously as possible. Our ordnance for these sorties would typically be nine GBU-12s, or a mix of GBU-12s and unguided Mk 82s, but we also used ten other symmetric and asymmetric loads according to mission requirements.'

Supporting the images which showed F-15Es carrying a range of ungainly looking load-outs, a third 'first' for the Strike Eagle occurred when a GBU-28, two GBU-24s and six GBU-12s were released in a single sortie.

NIGHT CAS

Much of the 'Bold Tigers'' action happened at night when the Taliban felt safest to move. 'Calls for support were often as a result of Northern Alliance troops flushing the Taliban out of hiding and forcing them to take to the open. Our radio chatter would be intense at times, and we were far from refining the art of night CAS', 'Fang' recalled. 'Spear' continued, 'the lead pilot or WSO would sometimes be talking to a FAC who was not fully trained in the art of directing air strikes, so we had a very busy environment up there. NVGs helped us, but most of our work was done with the TP'.

Occasionally, humidity and smoke obscured the TP's view and the FAC would 'walk' the F-15E's bombs onto the target with verbal

corrections ('next bomb 50 metres north of your last', etc.). 'When the target could be clearly identified, the two-ship element would discuss the placement of their bombs before actually running in on the target – we did not want the debris and smoke from one another's bombs to obscure the target', 'Spear' explained.

People, vehicles and convoys were the most frequent targets called in, and they were despatched with proximity-fused Mk 82s – the 'Bold Tigers' refrained from using CBUs due to the indiscriminate way in which this munition operates. Lt Col Britschgi recalled that for moving trucks, tanks and convoys, the GBU-12 was the weapon of choice;

'We became quite adept at hitting vehicles travelling at 60 mph with the GBU-12. We'd simply place our crosshairs in front of the lead vehicle, release the LGB and then walk the laser spot back onto the target.'

The GBU-12 was the precision munition most often employed not only because of its relative cheapness, but also because it did not exhibit a propensity for falling short of the target like some of the larger GBU series bombs. This was an important consideration when dropping weapons within close proximity of civilians or non-military buildings. 'We used new seeker heads to make sure that they worked right', Britschgi recalled.

Top and above
The flight from Kuwait to Afghanistan took several hours and a succession of air refuellings before the 'Bold Tigers' even reached the target area. Once in position, there was usually a 'vul time' lasting several more hours before the jets could return home. This led many of the squadron's sorties to exceed the ten-hour mark. Many of these missions took place during the hours of darkness (*Gary Klett via Author*)

The 'Bold Tigers' have traditionally been the most flamboyant decorators of all the F-15E units. The *"LET'S ROLL!"* badge was brought out across the USAF in memory of those who died in the attacks of 11 September 2001, but the colourful 'Bold Tigers' badge and tail flash are applied at the behest of the unit commander. The nose art applied during the 391st FS's deployment to Al Jaber invariably sought to honour the unsung heroes of '9-11' – most notably police and fire departments – but it was extremely interesting in that it also provided an instant tally of just how diverse a range, and large a quantity, of munitions were expended by the F-15E force during the course of the operation (*FJPhotography.com*)

When Troops In Contact CAS became necessary, the '391st' would venture down low to ensure maximum bomb accuracy and target identification confidence. Several times they struck Taliban troops who were so close that the FACs had to whisper their radio calls.

One example of enterprising tactics employed by the 391st FS involved a US Special Forces request for a strike on Taliban trucks, travelling in

convoy and about to 'requisition' a key bridge. The FAC, speaking in hushed tones, requested that the vehicles be hit without the destruction of the bridge over which the enemy was now swarming. The obliging F-15E pilot rolled his jet towards the bridge and decimated the Taliban convoy with several hundred rounds of 20 mm M56 High Explosive Incendiary. The bridge remained standing and was used later that day by the Northern Alliance to move reinforcements.

'The F-15E has employed the gun in combat before and it is a viable offensive weapon. Strike Eagle aircrew need to train to using it much more then every six months', 'Fang' commented.

Sometimes FACs used their own lasers for LGB work. 'The FAC would call a run-in heading, we'd synchronise laser codes so that our bomb "recognised" his laser beam and we'd roll in and pickle off a GBU-12, which the FAC guided to the target. It worked well', said 'Spear'. In these scenarios the GBU-12 was not only favoured for its ballistic properties, but also for its smaller explosive 'footprint', lest it go awry.

Some sorties resulted in frustration. All aircraft in-theatre were operating under strict ROE, especially those providing close air support. The 'Bold Tigers' took HQ-assigned ROE as a minimum criteria for weapons release and added their own discriminators to the equation, as 'Fang' explained:

'In all situations, targets had to be visually identified by the FAC as hostile. This had to be concurred by Lead and then by his wingman before we would strike a target. If either of the three decision makers had reservations, or could not see the target, weapons would not be released.'

Crews were genuinely concerned about the potential for innocent civilians being killed, and worked hard to ensure that this was avoided at all costs. 'Fang' cited a terrorist training camp by way of example;

'It measured 200 ft x 200 ft and was tasked for complete destruction. The limfac (limiting factor) was that it lay directly next to a mosque. We used GBU-12s to systematically demolish the camp, but left the mosque standing and untouched. As an added layer of protection, we only ever employed large weapons like the GBU-24 and GBU-10 2000-lb bombs when there was very little chance of collateral damage.'

The 'Bold Tigers' also flew reconnaissance missions (often at the behest of a FAC), and would scout roads and valleys for Taliban activity using the AAQ-14 TP. E-8C J-STARS aircraft were also in-theatre, although only a limited amount of work was accomplished with this particular platform.

Although showing a 17th Weapons School/57th Wing F-15E, this jet boasts the same load-out as carried by 'Crockett' flight for its record-breaking sortie, and also shows what a concurrent release of four GBU-12s actually looks like. The net result was that two buildings were simultaneously destroyed on a single pass (*USAF*)

LONGEST FIGHTER MISSION EVER

During the course of their three-month tenure, four 'Bold Tigers' entered the history books when they flew the longest fighter combat sortie ever – 15.5 hours (nine of which were spent over the target area).

'Crockett 51/52' was a two-ship F-15E flight tasked with patrolling a set of grid coordinates for the usual 'Vul' time of three hours. In the lead jet was 'Slokes' and 'Snitch' (pilot and WSO, respectively) and No 2 was crewed by 'Spear' and 'Buzzer'. Each F-15E carried nine GBU-12s, two AIM-9Ms, two AIM-120Cs and two wing fuel tanks. Once on-station, 'Crockett' flight received a TST from AWACS to contact a Predator UAV control unit. The latter had been monitoring suspicious activity around buildings believed to be Taliban command and control facilities. 'Spear' recalled;

'Each jet set up two different laser codes – No 1 had 1511 on the left CFT and 1533 on the right and No 2 had 1522 on the left and 1544 on the right. The lead pilot released four GBU-12s from his jet, giving us two with the 1511 laser code and two with 1533. We programmed in 1533 on our laser so that we could guide two of their bombs and they had 1511 dialled in on theirs so that they could guide two of ours. This way we took out two buildings, side-by-side, with simultaneous impacts for eight GBU-12s. We actually flew two passes – the first to ensure that we had the correct targets and the second to actually drop the weapons.'

Both targets were effectively neutralised. During the course of this action a lone AAA piece had been firing at the flight, and this too would have been attacked had it not been for the fact that the battery stopped firing at them and the F-15E crews were unable to locate it. One more building was subsequently struck and demolished following a second TST Predator tasking. 'Crockett' flight then pressed on with a road reconnaissance following a FAC call to request their help in identifying some vehicles that he had spotted.

Although unable to confirm the exact identity of the traffic, the flight soon came across a Taliban road block in the mountains and quickly despatched it. Having already air refuelled several times, the flight was taking fuel for their journey home when AWACS called them and asked them to contact Predator once again. A third building was assigned to them, and each jet rippled two GBU-12s into it. The building, suspected of sheltering Taliban fighters, was directly hit and destroyed.

'Crockett 51/52s" historic flight had seen the jets refuel no fewer than 12 times, each refuelling giving them an additional 60 to 90 minutes of loiter time. The mission had been hugely successful in terms of weapons delivery accuracy and weapons effects accomplished. Although the duration of the sortie was exceptional, 'Spear' seemed more impressed that his backside could still hurt a week later!

On 7 January 2002 the 366th AEW welcomed back the 391st FS from what had been a highly successful deployment, having been relieved at Al Jaber by F-15Es from the Seymour Johnson-based 335th FS. During the 391st's time assigned to OEF, it had achieved a sortie generation rate better than 85 per cent, flying between two and eight sorties every day for the duration of the deployment, each of which typically lasted between six and nine hours and involved anywhere up to a dozen aerial refuellings.

The tactics the 391st had used were heavily modified, and F-15E Fighter Weapons School (FWS) instructors have privately heaped praise on them for their innovation and success rate. 'Some of our most recent graduates did a fine job of "making things happen" in Afghanistan. Thinking through and executing "non-standard" tactics to achieve the

335th FS F-15E 89-0484 takes on fuel from a KC-10A en route to Afghanistan soon after the 'Chiefs' had replaced the 391st FS at Al Jaber in January 2002. The aircraft's GBU-10s, AIM-9Ms and AIM-120Cs are all visible in this photograph, as are the seeker heads for the targeting and navigation pods (*USAF*)

desired results is more important than mastering a single mission type – our boys made us proud', said FWS instructor 'Bud'.

'CHIEFS' TAKE OVER

As previously mentioned on 2 January 2002 the 'Bold Tigers' were replaced by the 'Chiefs' as part of the now-familiar AEF cycle. Mission rates and sortie types remained largely consistent throughout the 'Chiefs' rotation, the highlight of which was the debut of the BLU-118/B thermobaric bomb and the Battle for Roberts' Ridge.

Lauded by the international press as a grisly weapon that burned the oxygen from the lungs of its victims, the thermobaric bomb was seen as a solution to the Coalition's main problem at that time – flushing out Taliban fighters hidden deep inside a complex cave network built into the mountains.

The BLU-118/B is a penetrating warhead filled with an advanced thermobaric explosive that generates sustained blast pressures in confined spaces such as tunnels and underground facilities. The fill is made up of PBXIH-135, which is one of the US Navy's insensitive polymer-bonded explosives, and HAS-13, or SFAE (solid fuel air explosive). It is fused by the Fuse Munition Unit 143J/B, which has been modified with a new booster and a 120-millisecond delay. The BLU-118/B uses the same penetrator body as the standard BLU-109 weapon, and all BLU-109

Top and above
In the top photograph, a newly created BLU-118/B thermobaric warhead is carefully moved in preparation for its despatch to Al Jaber. In the lower shot, a 2000-lb GBU-24 is being hoisted into place in the bomb dump at the Kuwaiti base. This weapon is seen devoid of its GBU-24 Paveway III computer control and guidance unit, the latter only being attached when the bomb is made up for final fitment to an F-15E on the flightline (*USAF*)

weapon employment options warheads are compatible with the new BLU-118/B. The bomb's body can be attached to a variety of laser guidance system packages, including the GBU-15, -24, -27 and -28, as well as the AGM-130.

Employment techniques are said to include the following – vertical delivery, with the bomb detonated at or just outside the cave entrance; vertical delivery to penetrate and detonate inside the tunnel or adit; skip bombing with a short fuse to allow detonation at first- or second-impact (i.e. once inside the cave); and skip bombing with a longer fuse to allow penetration of a bunker door and maximum distance down a cave or adit.

On 3 March 2002 the first BLU-118/B was used against cave complexes in which al-Qaeda and Taliban fighters had taken refuge in the Gardez region of Afghanistan. Attached to the GBU-24 guidance and control kit, the weapon was assigned the GBU-24H/B designation. Unfortunately, the weapon missed the cave entrance and was unsuccessful, although this was not reported to the media. Planning the mission had revealed that the weapon's trajectory would have to be absolutely precise if it were to avoid a ridge that partly obscured the cave entrance. 4th FW pilot Capt Randall Haskin recalled;

'The margin for error was anticipated to be only 25 degrees. That margin was pretty small, all things considered. My Ops officer was at the CAOC when the mission was being planned, and they knew that there was a pretty significant possibility that it wouldn't work – a 50 per cent chance, if I remember correctly, was what he told the Commander who was overseeing the operation.

'The pilot performed a last second bunt to delay bomb release so that the WSO could get a better view of the DMPI – that's a normal thing for us to do with a standard LGB. With a Paveway III, however, the bunt put the bomb into a flight mode that was different to the one that had been planned, thus the bomb didn't follow the planned flight profile and smacked the ridgeline instead of the cave entrance.'

The automatic change of delivery occurred when the bomb sensed that it was no longer going to be dropped from a level attitude. Even though altitude had been lost in the bunt, it was the change in attitude from level flight to greater than five degrees nose-down pitch that caused the mode change and resulted in the ridgeline impact.

BATTLE OF ROBERTS' RIDGE

The other most notable event during the 'Chiefs'' rotation occurred on 4 March 2002 when a section of F-15Es operating as 'Twister 51' and '52' became embroiled in what is now known as the Battle of Roberts' Ridge. Flying in the lead jet were Lt Col James Fairchild (WSO) and Maj Chris Short (pilot), whilst Capt Kirk Rieckhoff (pilot) and Capt Chris Russell (WSO) manned the second Strike Eagle. Carrying a load of nine GBU-12s, two AIM-120Cs, two AIM-9Ms and 510 rounds of PGU-28 bullets, 'Twister' flight was four hours into an on-call

Pre- and post-impact photographs of the same test site in the USA showing the charred (but otherwise undamaged) entrance to a cave used during BLU-118/B thermobaric bomb trials in 2001 (*USAF*)

CAS mission when, at 0125 hrs, AWACS directed them to call 'Texas 14' immediately.

FAC 'Texas 14' talked them onto an observation position and suspected mortar sites on a ridgeline known as 'Whaleback'. Having dropped a single GBU-12 on the observation position, they received a call at 0141 hrs. A minute later, 'Mako 30' came on frequency and reported that he was taking mortar fire from positions west of him. He passed coordinates that 'Twister' identified as friendly, and when asked to confirm the location of the enemy, 'Mako' responded that he was unable to, adding only that opposing forces were 600 yards west of him.

By now it was clear to 'Twister' that 'Mako 30' was not a FAC or an ETAC (Enlisted Tactical Air Controller), as he made no attempt at the standard 9-line CAS brief. Instead, he reported taking fire and requested GBU-12s as soon as possible. 'Mako 30', it was later learned, was a SEAL (Sea Air And Land Special Forces) team searching for fellow SEAL Neil Roberts who had fallen from an MH-47E Chinook following an ambushed insertion in the Shah-i-Kot Valley. Lt Col Fairchild recalled;

'"Mako 30" reported that he was taking fire and needed air support, so we made two passes and dropped a GBU-12. He then called that he was still taking fire and was moving east with two wounded and one Killed In Action. Simultaneously, we were directed to clear the target area where Operation *Anaconda* was being fought – a B-52 was inbound to drop JDAM. We took advantage of this break to go get gas and rejoin the flight. "Twister 52" had already been sent to the tanker.'

The first GBU-12 dropped at 0153 hrs had fallen eight kilometres north of the ridgeline because of difficulties in confirming the target's exact coordinates. In short, the wrong coordinates were entered into the Strike Eagle's computer. During the effort to support 'Mako 30', a USAF

A US Army Special Operations Command MH-47E similar to this one was downed by an RPG in the Shah-i-Kot Valley during the second attempt to recover the body of Navy SEAL Neil Roberts on 4 March 2002. The grenade entered the open rear-entry ramp of the helicopter and exploded in the cockpit (*US Army*)

MH-47 carrying a second rescue team was downed by a rocket-propelled grenade. 'Mako 30', which had been making its way to Roberts' Ridge on foot, was situated atop a nearby peak, but the downing of the Chinook on the ridge itself soon resulted in a call for CAS from USAF SSgt Kevin Vance's ETAC team 'Slick 01'.

Coming off the tanker at 0237 hrs, 'Twister' flight was instructed to work with 'Texas 14' – a third team on a ridge line to the east of 'Slick 01'. 'Twister 51' employed three GBU-12s on the 'Whaleback' and 'Twister 52' dropped eight GBU-12s on the same target between 0252 hrs and 0303 hrs. One minute later they were then told to contact 'Slick 01' – Vance's crew from the downed MH-47, 'Razor 01'. Capt Chris Russell, WSO in 'Twister 52', recalled;

'They advised us that they were from the downed helicopter, and that they were taking fire from enemy forces that were within 75 metres of their position, so we basically knew we were going to be using guns only.'

Lt Col Fairchild added;

'Using the helicopter as a common reference point, "Slick 01" was able to talk us onto the enemy position using visual references and the TP. We made one 20 mm strafing pass at 0315 hrs, but were called off dry due to FAC calls that we were not on a good attack axis. We adjusted our run in and made more hot passes at 0320 hrs and 0323 hrs. "Twister 52" also made two passes – one dry and one hot – and reported bingo fuel. We again sent "52" to the tanker and talked to AWACS about getting more gun-capable aircraft on station, but with no luck.'

The gun passes had provided good suppressing fire for 'Slick 01', and 'Twister' flight expended 380 rounds between them. Russell recalled that 'the call we heard was, "Good guns! I can smell the trees!" We'd basically split the pines, and he was close enough that he could smell the sap. That's how close we were. We carry 510 rounds of PGU-28, so we had only enough for about five passes before we ran out of ammunition'.

Fairchild and Short followed their wingman to the tanker and received half a load of fuel, before returning to the target area at 0343 hrs for more hot gun passes, as the section lead explained;

'We heard "Clash 71" – a section of F-16s from the 18th FS – checking in on one of our radios, but then they checked off again. We went to the primary command and control frequency and were finally able to make contact with "Clash 71". Maj Short gave a fighter-to-fighter brief to "Clash 71", talking them into the target area. We passed the target to them and then headed to the tanker for a full load of fuel. We got back to the target area and "Clash" had already bingo'd out to the tanker. Both flights were "winchester bullets" (out of bullets) at this time, so we talked the FAC into letting us use GBU-12s by walking them in.'

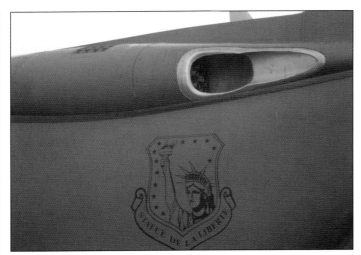

The gun port for the M61A1 Vulcan 20 mm gatling gun is located in the right wing root. It was not until 2001, and the use of the gun in OEF, that the F-15E community started to place additional emphasis on gaining some familiarity with the weapon in the air-to-ground environment. At the time the Battle of Roberts' Ridge was waged, three of the four flight members had never even fired the weapon before. The *STATUE DE LA LIBERTE* badge denotes that this is a 48th FW jet (*FJPhotography.com*)

A 492nd FS jet returns to Al Udeid, in Qatar, following an uneventful OEF sortie in 2004 (*USAF*)

At 0407 hrs 'Clash 71' made a hot pass with their guns, effectively covering 'Twister' flight's absence as they once again departed to the tanker for more fuel. Returning to the target area, 'Twister 51's' secure radio failed, and tactical lead was passed to 'Twister 52' to allow continued secure communications with 'Slick 01'.

Back on scene by 0445 hrs, 'Twister' flight was forced to remain away from the immediate vicinity of the target area while a Predator UAV reconnoitred the target area. At 0517 hrs 'Slick 01' requested 'Twister' drop their bombs a mere 200 metres west of the downed Chinook, and 'Twister' flight devised an impromptu plan to 'walk' their GBU-12s closer to 'Slick 01' until the target was hit or suppressed.

'Twister 52's' first pass at 0521 hrs, with 'Twister 51' in trail, resulted in a dry pass when clearance to drop was not obtained. Two minutes later, 'Slick 01' called again that he was receiving mortar fire and requested bombs on target immediately.

Struggling to understand the exact location of the friendly forces in relation to the enemy, the Predator attempted to elicit a more detailed mental picture through voice communications with 'Slick 01', and it is whilst conducting this dialogue that 'Twister' flight was directed by CAOC through AWACS to return to base (RTB). At 0526 hrs 'Twister 52' acknowledged the call, but informed AWACS that 'Slick 01' was still taking mortar fire and needed bombs on target quickly. This call was quickly followed by another request to fly a pass to support 'Slick 01',

The lethal radius of the GBU-12 500-lb LGB was in the region of 425 metres according to the 335th WSO Capt Chris Russell. The friendlies on Roberts' Ridge were so close to the enemy – in the region of 75 metres – that the possibility of fratricide from any of the F-15E's bombs was very real indeed. Use of the gun in these circumstances was the only viable option (*FJPhotography.com*)

which AWACS duly approved on the basis that 'Twister' flight would RTB afterwards.

With the situation becoming more desperate by the minute, the pace of events quickened. At 0529 hrs 'Twister 51' flew a target attack, but came off dry when his GBU-12 failed to release. 'Twister 52' then experienced communications jamming and also came off of his pass dry when permission to drop could not be obtained. Communication was resumed at 0532 hrs, and 'Twister' flight was cleared hot.

Over the next four minutes both F-15Es dropped a GBU-12, the first bomb landing 400 metres away from 'Slick 01' and the second only 200 metres. At 0540 hrs 'Twister' hit the

Patrolling over the rugged Afghan landscape, a 494th FS crew top off their tanks from a 22nd ARW KC-135R mid-patrol in 2004. Again, the F-15E carries the standard GBU-10/AIM-9M/AIM-120C load-out mix. Note that the aircraft has light grey F-15C drop tanks beneath its wings (*USAF*)

tanker for the final time and requested CAOC clearance via AWACS to return to drop their two remaining bombs. This was declined and the jets departed the area to return to Al Jaber.

'Twister' flight's total mission time was 12.3 hours, approximately six of which were spent in the target area. Follow-on support for the troops was later provided by B-1Bs, B-52s, Predator UAVs and AC-130 gunships. In his closing remarks, Lt Col Fairchild paid homage to these men;

'Those kids were on the ground for 15 hours before they were finally pulled out. People have made a lot out of what we did that day, but in my opinion the real heroes of the day were the guys on the ground fighting to stay alive. I don't remember all of their names, but the two people that stand out in my mind after reading accounts of what happened are the ETAC, SSgt Kevin Vance, who fought like hell that day, and Sgt Jason Cunningham, the PJ (para-jumper) who was killed while collecting casualties and treating wounded.'

The mission provided several learning points for the F-15E community, despite its overall success. Of these, the most pertinent was the need to confirm the plot of coordinates between aircraft – a requirement highlighted when the first GBU-12 missed the correct target by several miles. The need to coordinate deconfliction and optimisation of assets on scene – a near miss of less that 300 ft with a Navy P-3C Orion during one bomb run had occurred – was also apparent.

'Twister' flight later concluded that there had been 'less than optimum management of strike assets', and the 'utilisation of a weapon (M61A1 cannon) no one was fully trained on'. Out of the two four-ship qualified flight leads, an Instructor WSO and upgrading IWSO in flight, only 'Twister 51A' (Maj Short) had shot the gun before, and that was only once during F-15E conversion training! All four members of 'Twister' flight received the Silver Star for their gallantry.

AFGHANISTAN 2005

F-15Es continue to provide support to OEF at the time of writing. There is presently a lower level of conflict in Afghanistan today than there is in Iraq, meaning that the majority of F-15E sorties flown in the South West Asia region are tasked to OIF (see Chapter 6). Even so, the CAOC retains the ability to task sorties dynamically, enabling it to alter the balance flown in either Iraq or Afghanistan. 48th FW F-15Es flying from Al Udeid air base, in Qatar, have, for example, protected UN-sponsored reconstruction teams in Afghanistan one day and then flown CAS in Iraq the next. The Afghan elections of October 2004 were also supported by F-15Es.

48th FW Vice Commander CO Col James Brown checks the AIM-120C affixed to the wing pylon of his F-15E during the 494th FS's deployment to Al Udeid in 2004 (*USAF*)

OPERATION *IRAQI FREEDOM*

As President George W Bush made his intentions to implement regime change in Iraq clear in late 2002, it became obvious to even the most cautious observer that war with Saddam Hussein was imminent. The 4th FW, stationed at Seymour Johnson AFB, in North Carolina, and the largest F-15E Strike Eagle operator in the world, was initially notified in the last week of December 2002 that it had to have at least one squadron ready to deploy to the Persian Gulf region by early to mid January 2003.

The 4th FW's deployment was cryptically referred to as *Coronet East 074*, which was a code name for its deployment to Al Udeid air base, in Qatar. Al Udeid had been designed by the Qataris as an attractive basing point for USAF KC-135 and KC-10 air refuelling tankers, and it featured a 15,000-ft runway – the longest in the region. It was, however, not as well-suited to fighter operations as the advance survey party from the 4th FW Operations Group (OG) would have liked.

Arriving in late December to evaluate Al Udeid for Strike Eagle operations, the party discovered that the munitions dump was too small and that refuelling points clustered around the tanker operations areas were not going to be of much use to hordes of fighters flying high sortie rates. The OG fashioned a new, open-air, weapons dump, significantly increased the base's fuel capacity from one million to five million US gallons of aviation fuel and installed new 'hot pit' refuelling points across the flight ramp.

Of the two operational Strike Eagle squadrons at Seymour Johnson (there are also two training squadrons in residence at the base), the 336th FS 'Rocketeers' was selected to deploy first. Some 26 aeroplanes were readied (two were air spares), and between 11 and 17 January 2003 all 24 assigned aircraft successfully arrived in Qatar, via Moron air base, in Spain, where they had enjoyed a brief night stop for crew rest.

All pilots and WSOs were initially given inoculations against smallpox upon their arrival and then inducted into the current state of operations in the region. This essentially involved a briefing from the planners at the CAOC in Saudi Arabia (at Prince Sultan air base), where the battlefield of Iraq was being prepared under the auspices of OSW. The latter had by now metamorphosed into an operation that was oriented more towards gathering intelligence on enemy positions and strengths, as well as initiating regular punitive strikes against key Iraqi C3I sites and IADS nodes within the OSW area.

The Strike Eagle crews were initially unable to contribute to this preparatory stage as they remained firmly grounded at Al Udeid air base until 27 January, when the governments of the United States and Qatar

The 4th FW at Seymour Johnson is home to the largest contingent of Strike Eagles anywhere in the world, with four squadrons – two operational and two training – occupying a single ramp. The two operational squadrons deployed to OIF were supplemented by both instructor pilots and WSOs drawn from the 333rd and 334th FSs (*FJPhotography.com*)

finally concluded their diplomatic wranglings and permissions to fly were finally secured.

NTISR

When diplomatic permissions were eventually negotiated, F-15Es began flying non-traditional intelligence surveillance and reconnaissance (NTISR) missions. This involved using the aircraft's onboard sensors – LANTIRN pods, radar, Fighter Data Link and ZSW-1 Data Link pod – to scour Iraq for targets of interest. NTISR sorties were flown under the 'Strike Familiarisation' banner. SFAM meant that aircrew flew missions with live ordnance and with ROs ready to be executed should the CAOC send them the signal to strike while aloft.

These sorties were principally designed, however, to allow aircrew to familiarise themselves with ROE, local area procedures and flying over hostile territory prior to all-out war.

NTISR usually involved reconnoitring specific targets or areas of suspected activity, principally via the AAQ-14 or AAQ-28 FLIR targeting pods, but also using the APG-70 radar and the 'Mk 1 eyeball'. Intelligence personnel would then download the resulting pod/radar video and analyse it for tell-tale signs of Iraqi activity, passing the relevant clips of video up the chain of command to the CAOC for further expert analysis.

At this point in time the CAOC was still using the OSW system of dividing Iraq into large swathes of land named after US states. Thus, a crew might be assigned to conduct NTISR in the vicinity of 'Utah', for example.

When not flying, the 'Rocketeers' busied themselves preparing attack profiles against the 40+ targets that they would be tasked to strike on the first night of the war. They had initially been briefed in on the first six or so prior to leaving Seymour Johnson, and there was plenty of time to fine-tune their planning once in the desert.

SCAR

Within days of commencing flying out of Qatar, the 336th FS was formally asked to begin practising Strike Coordination Attack and Reconnaissance sorties (SCAR). Officially at least, SCAR was a new tasking for the men and women on the squadron, although a rendition of it had been implemented by the two F-15E units that had participated in OEF – the 391st FS and the 'Rocketeers'' sister-squadron, the 335th FS.

SCAR proved to be one of the areas in which the Strike Eagle excelled. In basic terms, this mission tasking placed the burden of responsibility upon the F-15E for finding, identifying, evaluating for collateral damage and handing-off targets to other strike platforms as they entered the area. It was very similar to the Forward Air Controller (Airborne) role, although fighter-to-fighter rather than 'slow-mover'-to-fighter, and without there being friendly troops in physical contact with the enemy. The US Navy's F/A-18s and F-14Ds had flown this 'Hunter/ Killer' role for a number of years.

Operating at medium altitude, the F-15E crew not only had to hand-off the target to the striker, but also perform a Positive ID (PID) to ensure the target was hostile. A Collateral Damage Estimate (CDE) also had to be carried out in order to quantify the likelihood of friendly or civilian casualties from bombing the target based on the known blast radii of the myriad weapons that might be employed. Not only did this place a huge responsibility on the crew, it was also a role for which the 336th TFS had never trained.

Teaching aircrew to do this in peacetime is a time-consuming and drawn-out process – it is even more impressive then that the 336th FS crews quickly embraced SCAR and became skilled at executing it.

As the unit engaged in SCAR practice, the CAOC tasked it with executing several high-profile OSW ROs. Unfortunately, some of these went awry and the CAOC – operating in a political spotlight of great intensity – reacted strongly.

On one occasion a 'Flat Face' EW radar on the Jordan/Iraq border was selected for destruction. Two Strike

Having seen action in OEF from Al Jaber in 2002, 335th FS F-15Es deployed to the region once again in early 2003 for OIF (*USAF*)

Eagles located the site, but the first did not drop due to weather over the target and the other mistakenly struck a re-supply building nearby. On another OSW mission, a 'Pluto' EW radar was targeted, but two flights of F-15Es failed to completely destroy it over the course of two separate strikes – a B-1B was tasked to hit the site with JDAM on the third night, which it did successfully. Whilst it is inevitable that misses will occur even with the best planning, ROE and circumstances beyond the control of the men and women in the F-15E cockpits had exacerbated the situation.

The 2000-lb GBU-10 was the munition of choice throughout the 1990s, and for the duration of ONW and OSW. Seen here with the seeker kit collar attached, but minus the seeker head itself, the basis of the GBU-10 – a bulky 2000lb LDGP bomb body – is self-evident. In OEF and OIF, the smaller 500-lb GBU-12 curried most favour with Coalition forces thanks to its better accuracy, lighter weight and reduced blast footprint, which minimised collateral damage issues (*FJPhotography.com*)

Despite the terse relations between the CAOC and the Al Udeid F-15E contingent for the remainder of OSW, the Strike Eagles continued to be called upon to fulfil key tasks in the preparation for war. Indeed, there were far more successes than failures, and the 336th FS struck radio relay stations, C3I posts, IADS nodes and leadership targets with alacrity. On one night alone, four F-15Es dropped GBU-24s into the Republican Guard/Baath Party HQ in Basra, whilst another four-ship flight flattened a nearby Air Defence Sector HQ with six GBU-10s.

PREPARATIONS CONTINUE

On 7 February, the 4th FW commander, Brig Gen Eric J Rosborg, arrived to take command of Al Udeid, which had grown rapidly and was now also home to F-16CJs, F-117s, Royal Australian Air Force F/A-18As, KC-135s, KC-10s, four US Navy F-14As and Royal Air Force Tornado GR 4s, in addition to the F-15Es. On the same day Operational Plan (OPLAN) 1003V was briefed to the 'Rocketeers'' resident pilots and WSOs. OPLAN 1003V defined how the Coalition would go about initiating full-scale ground and air operations to unseat the Iraqi dictatorship.

Towards the end of February the 336th FS received additional aircrew to bolster their numbers. The unit was now comprised of over 150 pilots and WSOs, many of whom were drafted in from the two fighter training unit squadrons at Seymour Johnson (the 333rd and 334th FSs) as well as the 391st FS at Mountain Home.

The increased intake had been expected, and was necessary to satisfy the 2.0 crew ratio ordered by the CAOC, which meant that there were four aircrew for every Strike Eagle in-theatre. As these crews continued to fly SFAM missions and conducted NTISR, the 335th FS 'Chiefs' at Seymour Johnson also deployed to Al Udeid, raising the total number of F-15Es at the Qatari air base to 48 jets.

Laser eye protection was one consideration that was given significant thought as the proposed start date of the war – 19 March – drew nearer. It was well documented in classified and open source reports that the threat of instantaneous or delayed blindness to aviators illuminated by lasers was real indeed. USAF Intelligence officers briefed the 'Rocketeers' and 'Chiefs' that Iraqi forces were using uprated commercial lasers, affixed to AK-47 assault rifles, to aim at aircraft passing overhead.

At least one F-16 pilot had suffered damaged vision following a sortie over Iraq in the years before, and some F-15E aircrew therefore elected to wear eye protection glasses which both squadrons had hurriedly sourced from a UK manufacturer.

Also new to both units was a limited supply of Northrop Grumman AN/AAQ-28 targeting pods – an enhanced version of the original Lockheed Martin AAQ-14 TP. The AAQ-28, which is better known as the Litening II Advanced Target Pod, features a laser spot tracker and optical sensor in addition to an improved derivative of the FLIR sensor from its predecessor. These additional systems allowed better daytime operation and extended range target acquisition capabilities, as well as facilitating coordination with other ground and airborne laser designators. However, the Litening II pod's IR sensor was inferior to the AAQ-14 in some respects, as shall be seen later in this chapter.

The new pod also required reduced maintenance support on account of the fact that it had no slip ring – the latter allowed the electronics and optical assemblies in the nose of the pod to slew freely in any direction. The slip ring had proven a maintenance nightmare in frontline service, and was replaced in the Litening II pod by a wiring loom that could be coiled to allow the optics in the nose to rotate freely, but which had to 'de-roll' once it had coiled/rotated more that 425 degrees.

Despite the increased supportability of these pods, there was a critical caveat that lessened their overall impact on the war. Unfortunately for the 4th FW, the wing was not permitted to maintain the AAQ-28 pods, as 335th FS IWSO Capt Christian Burbach explained;

'The technical representative from Northrop Grumman was the only guy allowed to troubleshoot them, and he could not get into the country for some reason. So, we had 18 or 19 of these pods, but between the two squadrons we had only 6-9 that actually worked!'

The de-roll process, which could occur without warning to the crew, would spin the seeker head back to its neutral setting to uncoil the wire bundle, and in the weeks to come at least one aircrew would be actively lasing a target with the bomb in flight when the pod decided to de-roll. 336th FS IWSO Capt Joe Siberski recalled;

'The de-roll bit me a couple of times. It wasn't like I didn't know about it, or that I wasn't checked out on the pod properly. The problem occurred when we were in dynamic targeting environments without a pre-planned attack and we executed a dive-glide or dive-toss attack. In a dive-glide/dive-toss attack, the pilot rolls inverted and pulls, which potentially does two things. First, (geometry dependant) the pilot may visually check the designation in the HUD. Second, diving at the target gives the WSO some extra time to acquire (or identify) the

An enhanced version of the original Lockheed Martin AAQ-14 TP, the AAQ-28 is better known as the Litening II Advanced Targeting Pod, and features a laser spot tracker and optical sensor in addition to an improved derivative of the FLIR sensor from its predecessor. These additional systems allow better daytime operation and extended range target acquisition capabilities, and also facilitate coordination with other ground and airborne laser designators. The new pod is externally distinguishable from the LANTIRN AAQ-14 TP through its revised array of cooling vents at the rear, a new cooling scoop on the side and a slightly more bulbous overall appearance (*FJPhotography.com*)

target in the pod so that we can deliver ordnance and not "go through dry" on the first pass. Getting a bomb off on each pass can be critical when gas is tight and the natives are restless.

'With a Litening pod, when you roll and pull, it wraps up the pod, and you can usually get down the chute, deliver the bomb and start the designator leg, but it will usually hit the limit some time before impact as you pass the target, causing a miss. We can bunt instead of rolling, but we don't normally like to bunt – negative G is bad, and stuff starts flying around the cockpit. It is more natural and more effective to roll.

'The roll limit can also bite you in a CAS environment where the "Wheel" tactic is used. Wheeling around the target area is more of a visual tactic, but I usually put the pod on the target, which would wrap up. To counter this, you can execute a "modified racetrack" or "bowtie" orbit. In conclusion, I thought the roll limit sucked, but we learned to cope with it and just not roll.'

One small bonus that Litening II brought to the WSO in particular was the manner in which the picture was orientated and rotated on the MPD. The image rotated within the display as to the aircraft's position relative to the target as it changed. Capt Siberski commented;

'It had something to do with the way the image is processed, coupled with the fact that the new pods had an internal INU (Inertial Navigation Unit) for tracking/coordinate reference. I didn't even notice it after a while, bit it gave me a little more situational awareness on how we were moving about the target when I was stuck heads-down at night.'

EW RADARS

The CAOC continued to task ROs in the final weeks of OSW. One particular objective was to take down Iraq's EW network on the border with Jordan – an important objective, as OPLAN 1003V required that USAF F-16CJs and Special Forces helicopters would operate out of Jordan once hostilities began in earnest (in fact, the earlier response options to target the 'Pluto' and 'Flat Face' radars had formed part of this objective). Accordingly, several radar sites and radio relay antennae were struck in the vicinity of H3 airfield and across the length of the border.

These missions were invariably met with heavy AAA opposition, and there were known SA-13 and Roland SAM sites whose weapon engagement envelopes protected the Strike Eagle's assigned targets. On one occasion three F-15Es flew west of H3 in order to bomb S-60 AAA and mobile Roland SAM batteries, and although the former were successfully dispatched, the SAMs escaped unharmed after AWACS passed the lead jet new coordinates in flight.

In the ensuing engagement, the new coordinates matched what looked like a Roland launcher, but the pod video later showed it to be a small hut of no military value. Post-strike satellite imagery revealed the SAM sitting safely in the original position briefed by the 336th's Intel officer!

The IrAF continued to fly its own continuation sorties within the sanctity of the airspace north of the 32nd Parallel and south of the 35th Parallel right up to OIF, MiG-23s, MiG-25s and Mirage F1EQs often venturing all the way down to the edge of the southern No-Fly Zone before crossing it briefly or heading back home well-short of the line. On more than one occasion, F-15Es flying DCA patrols were alerted to the presence of airborne threats and tracked them on radar (and FDL), certain that Iraq was about to launch its own pre-emptive attack against the Coalition. Nothing ever came of the IrAF's brief excursions south.

The complete lack of Iraqi air activity following the execution of OPLAN 1003V has prompted many to wonder if some kind of 'arrangement' with its leadership had not been secretly negotiated by US or British intelligence agencies beforehand, whilst others take the view that self-preservation simply took over within the IrAF once war started.

OIF COMMENCES

OIF came earlier than originally intended, and there remains a zone of confusion as to when OSW ceased and OIF commenced due to the fact that the procedures and ROE of the former were gradually phased out and replaced by the latter over the course of 24 hours.

It was immediately following a successful GBU-28 strike on the IOC at H3 by four F-15Es on 19 March that two F-117s headed north, at short notice, to strike a target believed to house Saddam Hussein. As the F-15Es returned from what will probably be classified as the last OSW sortie ever, their radios came alive and blocks of airspace were cleared by AWACS to allow passage for incoming Tomahawk land attack cruise missiles. As still more F-15Es made their way north to execute ROs and man DCA stations, they received word that their refuelling assets had been re-tasked (to support the F-117s, it later transpired) and they returned home early.

The first full day of the war (20th) saw experienced Strike Eagle crews tasked to launch AGM-130 strikes against key C3I and leadership targets, but the success of these raids is believed to have been adversely affected by EA-6B Prowlers conducting jamming operations in the vicinity of the

The GBU-28, in contrast to the GBU-10/12, is a deep penetration weapon useful for targeting command bunkers built underground. It was immediately following a successful GBU-28 strike on the IOC at H3 by four F-15Es on 19 March 2003 that two F-117s headed north at short notice to strike a target believed to house Saddam Hussein (*FJPhotography.com*)

Another 335th FS jet overflies southern Iraq in the immediate aftermath of OIF I. The aircraft is receiving fuel from a KC-135R (*USAF*)

The AGM-130 was a complex weapon to employ – so complex in fact that only qualified crews could use it. It offered the user several different flight profiles, allowing the weapon to be flown to the target with maximum efficiency, balanced with a minimum exposure to threat systems for the missile and launch aircraft. The weapon is seen here hung on an F-15E, decorated with messages from 'well wishers' to Saddam Hussein, and ready for the first night of OIF (*Randall Haskin via Author*)

target areas. Even so, great work was being accomplished by other F-15E crews as they began flying kill box interdiction (KI) and pre-planned precision strike sorties across the length and breadth of Iraq. Throughout the conflict, the Strike Eagle was the only airframe with the range, self-protection and target detection capabilities to enable it to roam freely over both northern and southern Iraq.

KI involved patrolling 30 x 30 mile grids that defined a kill box. SCAR missions were undertaken in these grids, and the F-15E often flew at medium altitude searching for targets of opportunity. When targets were found, the No 2 jet was usually the first to drop, as the section lead flew over and executed PID and CDE, then cleared No 2 – who was usually flying three miles in trail – to drop. This had the additional advantage of reducing No 2's weapons load, allowing him to save additional fuel. Wingmen typically burn more fuel than Leads because they have to manipulate the throttles more often to stay in formation.

Additionally, F-15Es carried a mixed load of fusing combinations on their GBU-12s – instant fusing on one side and delayed on the other – in order to operate as flexibly as possible in mixed-target environments.

The range of targets discovered and attacked is as holistic as it is impressive. The Strike Eagle is credited with destroying over 60 per cent of the estimated total force of the Iraqi Medina Republican Guard. F-15Es also scored direct hits on more than 65 MiGs on the ground. 4th FW jets also supported a great many Coalition infantry and armoured columns on the ground. Finally, the aircraft hit key IADS and C3I targets that often saw its crews fly deep inside the Baghdad 'Super MEZ'. The latter was the euphemism for the SAM threat rings encircling the capital, and which defined Iraq's thickest and greatest SAM threat.

The MEZ, which resembled the silhouette of Disney character Mickey Mouse's head, comprised Roland, SA-2, SA-3, SA-6, SA-8, SA-9 and SA-13 SAM systems, and the author heard of one report that at least one IHAWK SAM battery from the occupation of Kuwait 12 years previously was also active. Of course, for each SAM system there was a multitude of AAA of all calibres, including 100 mm.

Flying SCAR sorties worked out extremely well for the Strike Eagle, as it turned out. B-52s, B-1Bs, Navy/Marine Corps F/A-18s and F-14s and Marine Corp AV-8Bs all used the Strike Eagle to find, identify and hand-off targets to them. In 4th FW video footage taken during OIF and seen by the author, the two-person Strike Eagle crew is often heard working the radios hard – the WSO finding the target and talking the other platform onto it, and the pilot speaking to the AWACS and controlling the positioning of other strike fighters as they enter the area.

The cacophony of radio calls has to be heard to be believed, and one can only imagine the strain that these crews were under, particularly when the final responsibility for PID and CDE rested with them. It is a tribute to their professionalism that they achieved a number of 'firsts' whilst operating under these conditions. Perhaps the most noteworthy of these is what the author understands to be the first ever airborne buddy-lase of an AGM-65E laser Maverick missile, which was fired on command by a Marine AV-8B.

TASK FORCE *TAWNY*

The Special Operations Forces (SOF) campaign in Iraq, which was given the innocuous-sounding name Task Force *Tawny*, began long before OIF. However, once the war was in full swing, it was the 335th FS which provided the bulk of its airborne support, with the 336th FS also contributing to these operations from time to time. These highly-classified missions usually involved loitering within a 'black' kill box and communicating with ground operators over secure KY-58 radios.

The SOF troops typically carried covert IR strobes to allow the Strike Eagle crews to acquire them visually using NVGs, and they also operated their own laser designators to allow buddy-lasing of the Strike Eagle's LGBs. The SOF teams were most densely located in northern and western Iraq, where the 'Chiefs' spent much of their time.

Since the conclusion of the 'shooting war' part of OIF, more information concerning TF-20 missions has come to light. In particular, it now seems certain that they were run predominantly by civilian operatives, with support from trusted SOF troops. The TF-20 mission was primarily centred on the hunt for tactical ballistic missiles and the eradication of Baathist leadership figures.

When conducting operations with SOF, the pilot's or WSO's eyes were usually talked onto the target by the ground commander, although this sometimes proved much easier said than done. On one occasion a team of soldiers had come under fire from a group of Fedayeen militia in a pick-up truck. On foot and unable to give chase, the ground commander told the circling F-15Es to 'find and attack a white Toyota Corolla pick-up with blacked-out windows'. This was an impossible task for the Strike Eagle crew, whose TP simply could not discern such detail from the medium altitudes at which they were perched. With the soldiers on the ground in no immediate danger, the crew elected not to descend below the 10,000-ft minimum altitude imposed upon them by the wing.

When the situation became so precarious that a bomb could not be placed on target without the risk of hitting a friendly soldier, the F-15E employed its M61A1 Vulcan cannon to good effect. On one video the author saw of such an event, the SOF commander could be heard to say, 'Good rounds. That's got'em moving', as the 20 mm rounds impacted a tree line on the opposite side of the road from where he had taken refuge following an ambush.

On other occasions, SOF soldiers requested a show of force to try and flush out hiding loyalist fighters, which called for the Strike Eagles to fly highly-dangerous low passes right into the heart of the small arms envelope. Such passes were conducted down to 300 ft (at night), and usually required that the pilot not only fly directly over the enemy position, but that he also dump flares so as to ward the opposing forces off.

These 'cloak and dagger' missions often involved direct contact with the operators on the ground, but there were instances when SOF troops provided tip-offs via the CAOC or AWACS and Strike Eagles were re-tasked in-flight to kill TSTs. On one such tasking, a pair of F-15Es were assigned to destroy a number of Scud launchers hidden in the culverts underneath the main road running north-to-south from Baghdad. It was only once the crews had returned to base, having successfully killed the vehicles, that they learned from the CAOC commander, who called to congratulate them, that SOF observers had been within 1500 metres of the targets as their bombs went in!

It was whilst flying a KI mission north of Tikrit – possibly in support of SOF soldiers – that the only F-15E of the conflict was lost. Capt Eric 'Boot' Das (pilot) and Major William 'Salty' Watkins (WSO) were dropping ordnance on a target on 7 April when their aircraft impacted the ground. Das and Watkins were posthumously awarded both the Distinguished Flying Cross and the Purple Heart.

STEEL EAGLE

Steel Eagle was one of the more interesting projects to come out of the CAOC during the war. Once a classified 'black' project born out of the weapons research laboratories at Eglin AFB, *Steel Eagle* was a slender pod that housed acoustic sensors programmed to identify the acoustic signature of a Scud launcher as it passed nearby. The author understands that the device – of which only 35 were manufactured – had to be placed fairly close to the vehicle's anticipated route of travel (probably within 100 ft), and that it would transmit a radio signal when a match was noted.

The theory behind *Steel Eagle* is somewhat similar to the Vietnam-era project *Igloo White*, but its operation was somewhat flawed because the Strike Eagle's weapons com-

Little information pertaining to Steel Eagle has been released, but the author learned recently that trials of the sensor were conducted as a quick reaction programme by the 46th Test Wing at Eglin AFB, in Florida. A photograph seen by the author during a visit there showed an F-15E carrying six of the devices on the left CFT. The passage of time will no doubt see more information become available about this system (FJPhotography.com)

So hectic was the 335th FS's operational schedule in 2002-03 that some aircraft deployed to OIF still carried their OEF markings from the previous year. OIF mission tallies were simply overlaid onto existing bomb logs from OEF. 89-0483 was one busy Strike Eagle! The bombs with yellow stripes denoted a mission flown by a 336th FS crew, while those with green stripes were undertaken by 335th FS crews (FJPhotography.com)

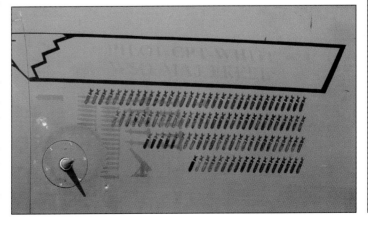

puter had no ballistics data with which to predict an accurate trajectory. Thus, it would have been impossible for the jet to have precisely placed the sensor. It is understood that of the 35 made, two were successfully dropped in tests at Nellis AFB by the 422nd Test and Evaluation Squadron, but the data derived from these drops merely validated the release characteristics of the sensor, and allowed it to be cleared for operational deployment. No *Steel Eagles* were dropped during OIF.

SNIPER AND OIF 2005

Perhaps the hottest topic of conversation within the Strike Eagle ranks today is the replacement pod for the LANTIRN AAQ-14. The Litening II pod certainly had its place in OIF, and added some capabilities to the Strike Eagle operations in the Iraqi desert, but it falls short of the expectations of those aviators who will be asked to take the Strike Eagle into the next war. The alternative to Litening II at the moment is the Lockheed Martin Sniper Extended Range (XR) pod.

Sniper XR should be up to ten times more accurate than the LANTIRN, with triple the recognition range and twice the resolution. It can acquire targets at altitudes of up to 50,000 ft, versus the 25,000 ft typical of the LANTIRN pod. Incorporating a high-resolution, mid-wave third generation FLIR, a dual-mode laser and a CCD-TV, along with a laser spot tracker/marker, Sniper should vastly improve target detection/identification capabilities. Capt Joe Siberski stated;

'I'm told that when we get Sniper, we will be able to obtain JDAM-quality coordinates. I'm also told that you don't have to depend on the EO camera on Sniper like we did for Litening. The Sniper IR picture supposedly compensates for light blooming and fires, and works like a "champ". How much fun would it be to have an F-15E, which can defend itself at medium altitude, passing coordinates to a data link-equipped bomber with a "bazillion" JDAM? While the bomber takes care of the fixed targets, the Strikers can get the movers with LGBs. I dare to dream! That's the main reason why we want a better pod, and Litening was sitting on the shelf when OIF kicked off. Now that it's over, the ANG can have their pods back and we'll take Sniper.'

And Siberski eventually got his way, for in December 2004 the

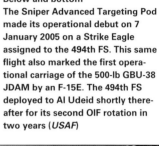

494th FS at Lakenheath received the first batch of Sniper pods assigned to the F-15E community.

Maj.Mike Neeman, who was one of the 335th FS crews at Al Udeid replaced by the 494th FS in December, explained that the mission types being flown in OIF today are reasonably predictable in nature;

'We usually fly NTISR, and we're basically acting as eyes in the sky for guys on the ground. We're at their disposal for CAS or battlefield interdiction as the requirement arises. We don't get a break, just like the guys on the ground, and we fly at various times during the day.'

Climate variations have a dramatic effect on the productivity of these missions. Capt Chris Torres approximated that during his AEF deployment with the 494th FS in 2004, almost half his sorties were cancelled due to weather. Neeman, on the other hand, recalled that very few of his were scrubbed due to the more clement conditions over Iraq at the time of his deployment. He added, 'We've seen the weather patterns here because we've been here quite awhile. Rarely were sorties cancelled, but sometimes they were less effective based on the weather'.

Neeman explained that the F-15E contingent in OIF remains coordinated with other fighter and support types also in-theatre, but that for the most part they operate over their own assigned geographical areas to spread the ability to react and respond to developments on the ground. There are, occasionally, exceptions to the rule, most notably the battle for Falluja in late 2004 when the 335th FS provided support to what was essentially a Marine-led operation. During this battle, Marine air power was the first port of call for both pre-planned and TST taskings, but the USAF's F-15Es and F-16s did drop ordnance during the operation.

AFTER THE SHOOTING WAR

When the 'Rocketeers' and 'Chiefs' returned to Seymour Johnson after OIF I, they were replaced by other F-15E units as part of the AEF cycle. In what has become known as the 'post-shooting war' phase, there was

Two 494th FS jets break away from their KC-135R tanker shortly after refuelling during an OIF II patrol near Baghdad on 28 August 2003. These aircraft carry identical mission load-outs – four GBU-12s, two AIM-9Ms, two AIM-120Cs and two underwing drop tanks (*USAF*)

much less activity in Iraq, and enemy resistance was sporadic and infrequent. As previously mentioned, Capt Chris Torres recalled that about 50 per cent of the sorties he flew were cancelled in 2004 due to poor weather in the kill boxes his unit was assigned to loiter over. Weather is not usually a factor for the F-15E, but with the primary mission being to support Coalition troops on the ground, a visual identification of each target is mandatory.

Lt Col Michael Arnold was assigned to the CAOC in Qatar between July 2003 and July 2004 as Chief of the Combat Plans Division, and he was responsible for planning the daily fighter sorties in both Afghanistan and Iraq. He explained;

'We'd frag all the aircraft to go and fill the required air strike requests from the Army, or we'd fill a contract with them that stated we'd have a set amount of CAS hours available to them at various times across the day. We passed this information along, but it was generally wide open, and there was not a great deal of specific planning for us to do.'

When Arnold and his team had completed their phase of the planning, the frag would be passed to the Combat Ops team, which would finalise specific details and disseminate the ATO to the flying units in-theatre;

'Everything was CAS after a certain point, because once the friendly guys were all over Iraq, there was no longer a forward operating line. We had to work to get close coordination and integration with the Army. You could say that everything that's happening in Iraq right now requires that close integration, and therefore qualifies as

A section of 492nd FS F-15Es close on their tanker during yet another OIF IV patrol in 2004 (*USAF*)

492nd FS jets leave Lakenheath at the start of their 2004 OIF IV det

CAS. That makes things simple in a way, but at the same time we've never actually fought a war that is totally in support of the troops.

'We make the plan as flexible as possible so that we can meet different potentialities, but there will always be limitations in resources. A ground commander might call for a jet with JDAM to drop on a house, but if there's only guys with LGBs up there then he'll have to either wait or make do with what he's got.'

Priorities were decided at the top of the chain of command and then filtered down;

'Sometimes Afghanistan took precedence over Iraq, depending on what was going on there. They'd say to us that they wanted a certain level of support in Afghanistan, but we'd have to play the game with the tankers – we can't send everything we've got if there's not enough tankers to maintain them.

'The Army would tell us how many sorties they wanted us to fly, and I would always respond by saying, "Don't tell me how much I need to fly. Tell me what effect you want, and I'll try and achieve that", because if I can achieve the effect by employing two A-10s, then I'm going to do that. It was a challenging joint issue when they'd be specific about this sort of thing. They'd also say, "We want you to fly your guys here, here and here", and I'd turn around and say, 'Well, you tell me what you want from us and I'll tell you where we can put our aircraft in the most efficient places to support you and get more productivity from the sorties.

492nd FS WSO Capt Mark Olguin checks the pop-out wings of one of his jet's four GBU-12's at Al Udeid prior to climbing aboard his F-15E and flying a CAS patrol over central Iraq in 2004 (*USAF*)

Not long after JDAM had been cleared for use by the F-15E, the 492nd FS became the first unit to carry the weapon in combat during its OIF rotation in the autumn of 2004. Here, the pilot of 97-0220 pumps out some flares as he breaks away from the tanker, revealing the solitary 500-lb GBU-32 JDAM attached to the jet's centreline station (*USAF*)

'For example, they'd be happy to have the jets sitting in a stack, not moving away from the immediate vicinity until they were called on. Although they'd be happy knowing they were there, we think that's an incredible waste of time. We could be using those flights of F-15Es, F-16s and A-10s to perform NTISR – looking for guys stealing copper from power lines, or checking out oil pipelines. Eventually, things got a lot better – the Army started telling us what they wanted from us, and we changed the way we did business in order to make it happen for them over Afghanistan and Iraq.'

Combat Ops had experts from each Major Weapons Systems community, allowing Arnold to analyse and evaluate other airframes' capabilities and potential;

'The more complicated the mission, the better it is to select an airframe with two seats. Just going out and dropping a JDAM is absolutely fine for the F-16, but when you have to fly a weapon into a cave, it becomes difficult to do that and control your own jet at the same time. On the other hand, the F-15E takes a lot of gas, and on occasion the biggest question was "how many tankers do we have available?"

'From a tactical standpoint, I think I'd take an F-15E every time. I think it has the best precision bombing and all weather capabilities. If you want JDAM the B-1B is fantastic, as is the B-52 – they carry loads and loads of them and go for thousands of miles without too much refuelling, but when you think about a CAS situation where you have to have the potential to put lots of ordnance on target, the F-15E is the best choice.'

APPENDICES

F-15E STRIKE EAGLE OPERATIONAL DEPLOYMENTS 1990 TO 2005

Year/Date	Squadron/Wing	Location	Operation	AEF
August 1990	4th TFW	Thumrait, Oman	ODS	
December 1990	4th TFW	Al Kharj, Saudi Arabia	ODS	
February 1991	335th TFS	Al Kharj, Saudi Arabia	OPC I	
January 1993	4th FW	Al Kharj, Saudi Arabia	OSW	
April 1993	48th FW	Aviano, Italy	ODF	
August 1993	492nd FS	Incirlik, Turkey	OPC II	
November 1993	494th FS	Incirlik, Turkey	OPC II	
February 1994	494th FS	Aviano, Italy	ODF	
October 1994	494th FS	Incirlik, Turkey	OPC II	
January 1995	494th FS	Incirlik, Turkey	OPC II	
July 1995	492nd FS	Incirlik, Turkey	OPC II	
1995	90th FS	Aviano, Italy	ODF	
1995	48th FW	Aviano, Italy	ODF	
June 1996	335th FS	Doha, Qatar	OSW	III
1996	492nd FS	Incirlik, Turkey	OPC II	
1996	391st FS	Incirlik, Turkey	OPC II	
February 1997	336th FS	Doha, Qatar	OSW	VII
February 1997	391st FS	Prince Sultan, Saudi Arabia	OSW	
April 1997	494th FS	Incirlik, Turkey	ONW	
August 1997	391st FS	Sheikh Isa, Bahrain	OSW	V
September 1997	494th FS	Aviano, Italy	ODG	
September 1997	492nd FS	Incirlik, Turkey	ONW	
March 1998	391st FS	Sheikh Isa, Bahrain	OSW	VII
December 1998	494th FS	Incirlik, Turkey	ONW	
January 1999	391st FS	Al Jaber, Kuwait	OSW	
January 1999	492nd FS	Incirlik, Turkey	ONW	
February 1999	494th FS	Aviano, Italy	OAF	
March 1999	336th FS	Incirlik, Turkey	ONW	
April 1999	336th FS	Incirlik, Turkey	ONW	
May 1999	492nd FS	RAF Lakenheath, England	OAF	
June 1999	492nd FS	RAF Lakenheath, England	OAF	
July 1999	335th FS	Incirlik, Turkey	ONW	
1999	391st FS	Sheikh Isa, Bahrain	OSW	
1999	391st FS	Incirlik, Turkey	ONW	
January 2000	492nd FS	Aviano, Italy	OJG	
May 2000	494th FS	Aviano, Italy	OJG	
May 2000	336th FS	Incirlik, Turkey	ONW	
December 2000	494th FS	Al Jaber, Kuwait	OSW	II
March 2001	492nd FS	Al Jaber, Kuwait	OSW	IV
October 2001	391st FS	Al Jaber, Kuwait	OEF	
January 2002	335th FS	Al Jaber, Kuwait	OEF	
June 2002	48th FW	Incirlik, Turkey	ONW	
February 2003	4th FW	Al Udeid, Qatar	OIF	
2003	492nd FS	Al Udeid, Qatar	OIF	
2003	494th FS	Al Udeid, Qatar	OIF	
2004	336th FS	Al Udeid, Qatar	OIF	
2004	492nd FS	Al Udeid, Qatar	OIF	
2004	335th FS	Al Udeid, Qatar	OIF	
2005	494th FS	Al Udeid, Qatar	OIF	

Key

ODS – Operation *Desert Storm*
OPC I/II– Operation *Provide Comfort I/II*
OSW – Operation *Southern Watch*
ODF – Operation *Deny Flight*
ONW – Operation *Northern Watch*

ODG – Operation *Deliberate Guard*
OAF – Operation *Allied Force*
OJG – Operation *Joint Guardian*
OEF – Operation *Enduring Freedom*
OIF – Operation *Iraqi Freedom*

COLOUR PLATES

1
F-15E 91-0306 of the 494th FS/48th FW, Incirlik AB, Turkey, 1997
Seen here in 494th FS/48th FW markings, 91-0306 was the 171st F-15E to be built (construction serial E171). It was delivered on 11 September 1992 to the 57th FW at Nellis AFB, in Nevada, where the jet was one of a dozen Strike Eagles assigned to the F-15E Fighter Weapons School (FWS). It remained at Nellis until August 1993, after which 91-0306 was delivered unmarked to the 494th FS at RAF Lakenheath on 12 October that same year. The jet still serves with the unit today. The load depicted in this profile – six CBU-87 Combined Effect Munitions (CEM) cluster bomb units and four GBU-12 500-lb LGBs – was typical of F-15E ONW load-outs in the late 1990s.

2
F-15E 91-0323 of the 494th FS/48th FW, RAF Lakenheath, England, 1993
The 188th (E188) F-15E constructed, this jet served with the 48th FW at RAF Lakenheath from 12 February 1993 through to 16 December 2002. In that time it participated in no fewer than ten operational deployments as part of OPC II, ONW, OSW, ODG, OAF and OJG. The F-15E has since been transferred to the 391st FS/366th Wing at Mountain Home AFB, in Idaho, where it remains today. Seen here carrying the GBU-15(V)1/2B, this long-chord wing version of the 2000lb IR- or EO-guided bomb has long been superseded by the short-chord GBU-15(V)21/22B.

3
F-15E 97-0218 of the 48th FW, RAF Lakenheath, England, December 1999
Delivered new to the 48th FW in November 1999, 97-0218 became the wing commander's jet, painted up in the flagship colours of the wing and bearing low-visibility renditions of the squadron badges from all three Lakenheath units on its left CFT (492nd, 493rd and 494th FSs). A standard peacetime training load is demonstrated here, including an AIM-120B AMRAAM and AIM-9M on the left and right shoulder pylons. The brown and yellow bands on the missile indicate the weapons' live rocket motor and warhead, respectively. Peacetime operations see captive rounds carried, and these feature blue bands instead.

4
F-15E 91-0603 of the 494th FS/48th FW, Al Jaber AB, Kuwait, December 2000
The 204th (E204) F-15E built, 91-0603 was a comparatively late arrival at Lakenheath, being added to the 'Panthers'' list of charges on 18 May, 1994. Loaded with two GBU-10 2000-lb LGBs, this aircraft participated in the 494th FS's solitary OSW deployment in 2000-01. Flying from Al Jaber, the aircraft helped police the southern No-Fly Zone over Iraq. OSW saw both pre-emptive and retaliatory strikes undertaken, although the latter ROs were usually of a punitive nature. This aircraft still serves with the 494th FS today.

5
F-15E 90-0251 of the 492nd FS/48th FW, RAF Lakenheath, England, 1998
Issued new to the 'Bolars' on 26 March 1992, 91-0251 (E153) is currently serving with the 57th Wing at Nellis AFB in support of the Weapons Instructor Course (formerly FWS). The aircraft was the 492nd FS flagship twice (in 1993-94 and from September 1997 to August 1999) prior to its departure from Lakenheath void of unit tail markings on 17 December 1999.

6
F-15E 98-0135 of the 492nd FS/48th FW, Al Udeid AB, Qatar, 2003
This aircraft was slated as the last ever F-15E for the USAF until an unexpected order for ten additional airframes was placed in 2000. Arriving at Lakenheath on 26 August 2000 following USAF acceptance trials three months earlier, 98-0135 (E226) is profiled here carrying an AGM-130 EO/IR-guided 2000-lb bomb. Also noteworthy is the associated AN/AXQ-14 data link pod on the central station. The jet is still assigned to the 492nd FS.

7
F-15E 87-0198 of the 391st FS/366th Wing, Al Jaber AB, Kuwait, late 2001
The 38th (E38) F-15E built, 87-0198 was delivered to the USAF on 15 May 1989 and eventually issued to the 336th TFS/4th TFW at Seymour Johnson AFB, North Carolina, in March of the following year. One of the first Strike Eagles to be delivered to the 'Rocketeers' as an F-4E replacement, the jet was passed onto the 335th TFS in October 1990 for the unit's imminent deployment to Operation Desert Shield. It duly flew 45 combat sorties during Operation Desert Storm, and was eventually passed on to the 391st FS at Mountain Home AB in August 1993. 87-0198 saw further combat with the 'Bold Tigers' in OEF, during which time it accumulated an impressive tally of mission markings – including single GBU-15 and GBU-28A symbols – and NYPD nose art, in addition to the '9-11'-inspired artwork that was applied to all 391st FS jets. Written below the nose art were the words Texas 12. Shown here carrying a GBU-28A LGB, this aircraft was reassigned to the 90th FS/3rd Wing at Elmendorf AFB, in Alaska, in mid 2002.

8
F-15E 87-0204 of the 391st FS/366th Wing, Al Jaber AB, Kuwait, late 2001
The 44th (E44) F-15E built, this Strike Eagle is also a Desert Storm veteran. It was delivered new to the 336th TFS in October 1989, having initially

been accepted by the USAF three months earlier on 11 July. The jet deployed to Oman with the 'Rocketeers' in August 1990, saw extensive combat and duly returned home in April 1991. Transferred to the recently reactivated 391st FS in October 1992, the F-15E experienced further combat with this unit in OEF between October 2001 and January 2002, when it dropped a GBU-28A, two GBU-10s and a succession of GBU-12s. 87-0204 was reassigned to the 90th FS at Elmendorf in March 2002, and it presently remains in Alaska.

9
F-15E 90-0227 of the 391st FS/366th Wing, Al Jaber AB, Kuwait, late 2001

F-15E 90-0227 (E129) was issued new to the 57th FW on 16 June 1991, and it would remain with this unit for nearly a decade. In the years that followed, the jet carried FWS and Weapons School markings until April 1993, when it became the 57th FW flagship. The aircraft filled this role until July 2000, when it was transferred to the 391st FS. Deploying with the squadron to Al Jaber for OEF in October 2001, 90-0227 dropped a large number of GBU-12s, two GBU-10s and two Mk 82 500-lb LDGPs during the campaign. It currently resides at Elmendorf AFB with the 90th FS, having been transferred to the unit in May 2002.

10
F-15E 87-0207 of the 391st FS/366th Wing, Al Jaber, Kuwait, 2001

Yet another *Desert Storm* veteran and ex-336th and 335th FS jet, 87-0207 was the 47th (E47) Strike Eagle to roll off the McDonnell Douglas production line in St Louis, Missouri. Delivered to the USAF on 8 August 1989, it was subsequently assigned to the 'Rocketeers' in October of that same year. Exactly 12 months later the jet was passed on to the 'Chiefs', with whom it saw combat over Kuwait and Iraq in January-February 1991. Transferred back to the 336th TFS in April 1991, 87-0207's somewhat nomadic existence continued 14 months later when it was flown to Mountain Home AFB for service with the 391st FS. A veteran of OEF, the jet returned home in January 2002 sporting myriad mission markings, including a GBU-28A and three GBU-10 drops. 87-0207 also dropped several GBU-15s during OEF, and one is seen here on the shoulder pylon in this profile. Like all 391st FS OEF jets, it was transferred to the 90th FS at Elmendorf following its participation in the campaign – it left the unit in February 2002.

11
F-15E 87-0182 of the 391st FS/366th Wing, Al Jaber, Kuwait, 2001

Seen here carrying a GBU-24 Low Level LGB, early-build (E22) 87-0182 was first assigned to the 336th TFS at Seymour Johnson in April 1989 following delivery for acceptance testing on 30 January that same year. The aircraft participated in *Desert Storm* with the unit and was then transferred to the 334th FS – the F-15E

Replacement Training Unit (RTU) – upon its return to Seymour Johnson. In October 1993 the jet was reassigned to the 391st FS and subsequently became the 366th Wing flagship until July 1998. A visit to Warner Robins AFB for planned depot maintenance took place in October 1999, after which the jet was repainted in standard 'Bold Tigers' markings. 87-0182 deployed to Kuwait for OEF and returned home wearing only the standard '9-11' nose art. It has been operated by the 90th FS at Elmendorf since May 2002.

12
F-15E 87-0210 of the 391st FS/366th Wing, Mountain Home AFB, Idaho, 2002

87-0210 (E50) rolled off McDonnell Douglas's St Louis production line on 5 September 1989 and entered service with the 336th TFS at Seymour Johnson AFB the following month. It deployed to the Persian Gulf in August 1990 and returned to North Carolina in April of the following year. By month-end the combat veteran had been passed on to the 334th FS, where it served with the RTU until handed over to the 391st FS in March 1993. It was the last aircraft to carry 366th Wing markings prior to the F-15E swap that took place between the 391st and 90th FSs in February-May 2002.

13
F-15E 90-0245 of the 90th FS/3rd Wing, Aviano AB, Italy, 1995

One of 20 brand new F-15Es delivered to the 90th FS between August 1991 and April 1992, this aircraft (E147) arrived at Elmendorf on 16 January 1992. It remained in Alaska for 11 years until transferred to the 391st FS at Mountain Home AFB in February 2003. 90-0245 is depicted here carrying four GBU-12 500-lb LGBs during the unit's sole operational deployment to date – the 1995 Operation *Deny Flight* detachment to Aviano AB in support of UN Resolutions 816, 836 and 958.

14
F-15E 90-0253 of the 90th FS/3rd Wing, Aviano AB, Italy, 1995

Resident at Elmendorf since 11 June 1992, 90-0253 (E155) was another of the 90th FS jets to deploy to Aviano in 1995. As a unit controlled by the USAF's Pacific Air Forces Command, the 90th FS was exempt from Air Expeditionary Forces (AEF) deployments until 2002. The squadron's primary remit is to support operations in the Pacific region, and it deploys regularly to South Korea for exercises as part of this role. The 90th FS has, therefore, only undertaken one AEF deployment (to Aviano) to date. This aircraft was acquired by the 391st FS in January 2003.

15
F-15E 87-0181 of the 336th FS/4th FW, Al Udeid AB, Qatar, March-April 2003

The nose art on 87-0181 *Lady Katherine* was applied by SSgt Nelson Ortega during the jet's OIF deployment in 2003. Delivered to the USAF on 7

March 1989 as the 21st (E21) F-15E built, the jet was assigned to the 4th TFW in May of the same year. It was the wing flagship until it deployed to Iraq with the 'Rocketeers' in August 1990, and the F-15E remains in service with the 336th FS today.

16
F-15E 89-0503 of the 336th FS/4th FW, Al Udeid AB, Qatar, March-April 2003
Delivered to the USAF on 8 March 1991, 89-0503 (E125) joined the 4th TFW two months later. Having missed out on *Desert Storm*, it saw combat in OIF as the 336th FS's flagship. The jet's *Taz* artwork was applied by A1C Ryan Stafford.

17
F-15E 88-1686 of the 335th FS/4th FW, Al Udeid AB, Qatar, 2003
POW-MIA is another of A1C Ryan Stafford's creations. This aircraft carried a single Mk 82 LDGP and a series of GBU-12 bomb markings post OIF. Delivered on 22 December 1989, the jet (E70) completed 52 missions with the 335th TFS 'Chiefs' in *Desert Storm*. Transferred to the 334th FS 'Eagles' in January 1992, it returned to the 'Chiefs' just three months later, and it remains in the unit's custody at the time of writing.

18
F-15E 89-0473 of the 335th TFS/4th TFW, Al Kharj AB, Saudi Arabia, March 1991
89-0473 (E95) was delivered to the USAF on 30 June 1990 and entered service with the 4th TFW four months later. The aircraft has enjoyed spells with all four squadrons at Seymour Johnson (333rd, 334th, 335th and 336th FSs), serving both as an operational and instructional airframe. It is depicted here carrying CBU-89 CEM as part of Operation *Provide Comfort I* in 1991. The jet is presently assigned to the 333rd FS.

19
F-15E 87-0209 of the 336th TFS/4th TFW, Al Kharj AB, Saudi Arabia, January 1991
Accepted by the USAF on 18 August 1989, 87-0209 (E49) was issued to the 'Rocketeers' 12 months later and immediately deployed with the squadron to *Desert Shield*. It returned to Seymour Johnson AFB in April 1991 and was transferred to the 391st FS in September 1992. An OEF veteran with the latter unit, the aircraft is now operated by the 90th FS at Elmendorf AFB. Seen here in *Desert Storm* configuration, the jet lacks an AAQ-14 TP.

20
F-15E 88-1686 of the 335th TFS/4th TFW, Al Kharj AB, Saudi Arabia, January 1991
The same aircraft as depicted in profile 17, but seen here 12 years earlier, 88-1686 served as the 335th TFS flagship following its delivery to the unit in October 1990. Boasting an unusual *Desert Storm* load-out of four GBU-10 2000-lb LGBs, the aircraft was the 'Chiefs' second most prolific bomber of the campaign.

21
F-15E 89-0487 of the 335th TFS/4th TFW, Al Kharj AB, Saudi Arabia, January 1991
The only F-15E to have scored an air-to-air kill, *"Lucky"* is depicted here prior to its victory. On 14 February 1991, the jet scored a direct hit on a Mi-24 'Hind' helicopter gunship as it threatened US Special Forces deep inside Iraq. Capts Richard Bennett (pilot) and Dan Bakke (WSO) 'pickled' a single GBU-10 at their hovering target some six miles away – they had been called in by AWACS to support the Special Forces squad after they had reported seeing several Iraqi helicopters off-loading troops in their immediate vicinity. Acquisition of the 'Hind' had come first from the radar, but a visual tally through the AAQ-14 TP quickly followed. Neither man was sure that the bomb would be able to hit the helicopter, but to their relief the Mil-24 vapourised some 30 seconds after the huge 2000-lb LGB had left their aircraft. The USAF did not officially recognise the kill until 2 November 2001. Block 47 (E109) airframe *"Lucky"* has always served with the 335th FS, and it dropped a further 100 bombs whilst flying with the unit in OIF. It is shown here carrying a mixed load of Mk 20 Rockeye CBUs on the right CFT and AIM-7M Sparrows on the left CFT.

22
F-15E 88-1672 of the 336th TFS/4th TFW, Al Kharj AB, Saudi Arabia, January 1991
88-1672 (E56) was delivered new to the 336th TFS in November 1989, and it is depicted here in typical *Desert Storm* configuration with 12 Mk 82 500-lb LDGPs attached to its CFT pylons. Due to the 'Rocketeers'' limited supply of AAQ-14 TPs in-theatre at this time, LDGPs were carried for the majority of the war by 336th TFS jets. Also an OIF veteran, 88-1672 has served exclusively with the 336th TFS for the past 16 years.

23
F-15E 88-1691 of the 336th TFS/4th TFW, Thumrait AB, Oman, October 1990
This was the archetypal load out for F-15Es sitting at Thumrait during *Desert Shield*. The 12 Mk 20 Rockeye CBU each boasted 500 lbs of anti-armour bomblets that were used against all manner of targets. This jet (E75) was delivered new to the 336th TFS on 3 April 1990, and has since served with both the 335th and 334th FSs. It is currently flown by the latter unit.

24
F-15E 88-1675 of the 336th FS/4th FW, Al Udeid AB, Qatar, April 2003
SNEAKY CARROT was the brainchild of SSgt Jason Henton, and it returned from OIF carrying one GBU-24 and five GBU-12 bomb markings. The jet (E59) was delivered to the 336th TFS on 1 November 1989, and it deployed to the Persian Gulf with the 'Rocketeers' in August 1990. The F-15E later flew with the 'Chiefs', before returning to the 336th FS, where it continues to serve today.

INDEX

References to illustrations are shown in **bold**. Plates are shown with page and caption locators in brackets.